AF701899

Palgrave Studies in Economic History

Series Editor
Kent Deng
London School of Economics
London, UK

Palgrave Studies in Economic History is designed to illuminate and enrich our understanding of economies and economic phenomena of the past. The series covers a vast range of topics including financial history, labour history, development economics, commercialisation, urbanisation, industrialisation, modernisation, globalisation, and changes in world economic orders.

More information about this series at
http://www.palgrave.com/gp/series/14632

Tirthankar Roy

How British Rule Changed India's Economy

The Paradox of the Raj

palgrave
macmillan

Tirthankar Roy
Department of Economic History
London School of Economics
London, UK

Palgrave Studies in Economic History
ISBN 978-3-030-17707-2 ISBN 978-3-030-17708-9 (eBook)
https://doi.org/10.1007/978-3-030-17708-9

© The Editor(s) (if applicable) and The Author(s), under exclusive licence to Springer Nature Switzerland AG 2019
This work is subject to copyright. All rights are solely and exclusively licensed by the Publisher, whether the whole or part of the material is concerned, specifically the rights of translation, reprinting, reuse of illustrations, recitation, broadcasting, reproduction on microfilms or in any other physical way, and transmission or information storage and retrieval, electronic adaptation, computer software, or by similar or dissimilar methodology now known or hereafter developed.
The use of general descriptive names, registered names, trademarks, service marks, etc. in this publication does not imply, even in the absence of a specific statement, that such names are exempt from the relevant protective laws and regulations and therefore free for general use.
The publisher, the authors and the editors are safe to assume that the advice and information in this book are believed to be true and accurate at the date of publication. Neither the publisher nor the authors or the editors give a warranty, expressed or implied, with respect to the material contained herein or for any errors or omissions that may have been made. The publisher remains neutral with regard to jurisdictional claims in published maps and institutional affiliations.

Cover illustration: Pictorial Press Ltd/Alamy Stock Photo

This Palgrave Pivot imprint is published by the registered company Springer Nature Switzerland AG
The registered company address is: Gewerbestrasse 11, 6330 Cham, Switzerland

To
Mrinmoyee Roy
because debates are fun!

Preface

How did British colonial rule (about 1765–1947) change India's economy? Those who wish to find an answer to this question have two choices.

First, they can read books and articles that tell a story. The story is this: the British government extracted resources from India and insisted on foreign trade being free, which helped British industry and damaged Indian industry. The policy enriched Britain and impoverished India. Thus, colonialism reduced a rich region to poverty. The advocates of this narrative include a collection of Marxists, politicians who write books, blog-writers, and economists seeking the holy grail of an explanation of world inequality.

Second, they can read books and articles the historians of India write, which are more reliably evidence-based than the former set and reject many of the claims the former set makes: for example, that India was once a prosperous land, or that the state extracted resources. But this scholarship does not suggest another paradigm. It goes deep into the working of the state and the economy, so deep that it loses its way in detail. Few of these works get noticed.

This book steps in to meet the gap that the historians leave behind. It is evidence-based, and it tells a story. What story is that?

The evidence tells us three things. First, the open economy that the regime sponsored delivered two extraordinary benefits to the Indians: it stimulated business and reduced deaths from diseases and famines. Second, the state's fiscal capacity was too small for it to make a difference in any other way. And third, some of the most stressed peoples in the region—most peasants, the oppressed castes, and women—did not become better-off in this time. They needed the state, but the state was not there for them. The story is that colonialism led to more inequality while it helped capitalism flourish. The book shows why the outcome of colonialism was such a paradoxical mixture of success and failure.

I use my own published scholarship as the primary ingredients to write this narrative. My debts are many. Most of these have been acknowledged elsewhere, except one. I warmly thank the readers for the press and the editor of the Palgrave Economic History series, Kent Deng, for their endorsement of the project and suggestions for improvement.

London, UK Tirthankar Roy

Contents

1	Introduction	1
2	The Making of British India	25
3	The Business of the Cities	55
4	Unyielding Land	81
5	A Poor State	99
6	End of Famine	111
7	A Different Story? The Princely States	135
8	Conclusion	151
Index		155

List of Figures

Fig. 1.1 Structural change: Business growth and agricultural stagnation. National income (million Rs., left) and income per worker (Rs. per head, right) by activity, 1938–1939 prices 11
Fig. 1.2 Population transition. Average population growth rate (% per year per decade) with a trend line added 12
Fig. 2.1 Tombs of early English settlers in Surat. A nineteenth-century photograph showing ruins of the graveyard of European traders who came to Surat from the seventeenth century and died in the city, the main port on the western coast. European settlement in this port (as in Masulipatnam on the Coromandel coast and Cochin in the deep south, which are the homes to Dutch graveyards) was small in scale, but of long duration (© DeGolyer Library, Southern Methodist University, William Johnson Photographs of Western India) 32
Fig. 2.2 Opium warehouse in Patna (1882). Looking like library stacks, the storage space shows the immense scale of the trade from eastern India and the extent of the government's involvement in it (© Artokoloro Quint Lox Limited/Alamy Stock Photo) 42
Fig. 2.3 Advertisement in a Bombay journal, 1845 44
Fig. 2.4 House of Forbes. The photograph shows the offices of one of the larger European trading firms of early nineteenth-century Bombay, and a partner

	of the Company administration in the city (© DeGolyer Library, Southern Methodist University, William Johnson Photographs of Western India)	45
Fig. 2.5	American Civil War Interrupted England's Cotton Supply. This cartoon from the 1860s shows a confused British merchant watching the battle in the United States, while a patient Indian trader stands in front of a cotton depot waiting to be noticed (© World History Archive/Alamy Stock Photo)	46
Fig. 3.1	Trade volume (million tons cargo through railways and ports)	56
Fig. 3.2	Transporting tea. Assam was remote and badly connected when tea plantations started there. This undated photograph shows the dependence of the trade on slow modes of transport of a delicate merchandise like tea. Railway connection running through present-day Bangladesh made for a revolutionary change (© PR Archive/Alamy Stock Photo)	64
Fig. 3.3	Grant Medical College in Bombay. Established in 1845 with a donation from Jamsetjee Jejeebhoy and the Governor of Bombay, Robert Grant, this was one of the first medical colleges in India (© DeGolyer Library, Southern Methodist University, William Johnson Photographs of Western India)	75
Fig. 3.4	A view of a woman spinning outside a hut, about 1860. A rare photograph of hand-spinning shows the conditions in which the industry carried on: part-time work by women, poverty, and the simplicity of the tools. Mechanized production replaced this type of work easily, which helped the users of cotton yarn but destroyed jobs of poor women (© British Library Board)	77
Fig. 4.1	Jat landholders, about 1890. This illustration of a group of cultivators from northern India is one example of a set of photographs made of occupational groups for circulation in Britain (© IndiaPicture/Alamy Stock Photo)	88
Fig. 6.1	Famine 1900. One of the last great famines, the 1899–1900 famine recorded a high death rate from diseases (© Photo 12/Alamy Stock Photo)	118
Fig. 6.2	Women workers in industry 1901–1991 (Undivided India till 1961, Indian Union after 1961)	126
Fig. 6.3	The ratio of women-men work-participation rate (%)	126

Fig. 6.4 Mother India (1957). Mother India was a retort to Katherine Mayo's infamous book of the same name published thirty years before (Chapter 1). The film celebrated the courage of a woman and her family against adversities and the harassments of an evil moneylender. At the time this proud patriotic statement about Indian womanhood appeared, Indian womanhood was doing badly, married in their teens, shut out from paid work by migrant men, and minding more children than a generation before (© TCD/Prod.DB/Alamy Stock Photo) 127
Fig. 6.5 Men of the Royal Air Force feeding local children, 1943. The job of feeding soldiers aggravated the 1943 famine in Bengal. Soldiers, however, took an active part in famine relief (© Trinity Mirror/Mirrorpix/Alamy Stock Photo) 128
Fig. 7.1 'Native Durbar' (1855–1862). This photograph of a royal court or durbar in session somewhere in Western India reminds us that, except for about five or six, the 500-odd princely states in India were little more substantial than the estate of a village landlord (© DeGolyer Library, Southern Methodist University, William Johnson photographs of Western India) 138
Fig. 7.2 The arrival of the first train in Alwar station, nineteenth-century. Princely states (like Alwar) emulated British India and built railways, hiring foreigners to run the system. With the small resources and territories that most of them had, the railways were usually short-haul narrow-gauge lines feeding into the main lines (© World History Archive/Alamy Stock Photo) 142

Map 2.1 Geographical zones. The map also shows major railway routes connecting the interior with the port cities from around 1880 27
Map 2.2 British India and the princely states (shaded) 35
Map 2.3 Types of land settlement, 1858 39
Map 4.1 Rainfall 96
Map 7.1 Major princely states 136

List of Tables

Table 4.1	Agricultural production, land area, productivity (annual percentage growth rate, British India, 1891–1946)	86
Table 4.2	Irrigated area as a proportion of cultivated area 1885–1938 (%)	97
Table 7.1	British India and states, 1905	141

CHAPTER 1

Introduction

Abstract How did British colonial rule shape India's economy? The answers to this question now available from academic and popular history are not always satisfactory, because these works do not clearly say what facts we should be explaining. The most important element of British economic policy was openness, or the desire to keep the borders open to movements of goods, capital, skills, and technologies. Openness delivered mixed results. It helped businesses grow and end famines, but did not help much the resource-poor countryside. Openness benefited men more than women, capital more than labour, and the upper castes more than others. The legacy of the regime, therefore, was a mix of successes and extraordinary failures. The book shows how this paradox can be explained.

Keywords Colonialism · British rule in India · Economic development of India · The Raj · Economic history

The Paradox of the Raj[1]

On an October morning in 1943, a scientist employed by the Government of Bengal was travelling by boat along the Brahmaputra river from Bahadurabad port to join his new job in Dhaka (now the capital of Bangladesh). All along the 120-mile journey, the horrified young man saw bodies of dead and dying men, women and children on both

© The Author(s) 2019
T. Roy, *How British Rule Changed India's Economy*,
Palgrave Studies in Economic History,
https://doi.org/10.1007/978-3-030-17708-9_1

banks of the river. Hundreds of them. There was a war on, and the enemy was within a few hundred miles to the east. But these people did not die in the war. They were victims of a famine that had begun in the summer months of 1943 and continued until the end of the year. When the famine ended, anywhere between one and three million people had died of starvation and diseases.

A colossal disaster as this one was, the Bengal Famine was an insignificant event when compared with the three famines that visited the Deccan Plateau in southern India between 1876 and 1899. Unlike the Bengal Famine, the Deccan famines happened in peace times; and unlike fertile well-watered Bengal, happened in a vast semi-arid subtropical region where lives depended on the timely arrival of the monsoon rains. If the rains failed in the two successive seasons, July and December, a famine condition developed. The mighty British Indian state, the Raj, was responsible for delivering relief, a job it did poorly. So poorly that the Deccan famines symbolized, for some, the British rulers' indifference to Indian people. Forty-four years later, The Bengal Famine revived the same negative image. A despotic and callous regime busy with its own warfare did not bother with relief. Famines, in one reading, represented the regime's capacity to tolerate and inflict violence.[2]

Nationalist critics of British India used the example of the famines to allege that the regime's economic policy had caused poverty to increase. The Bengali civil servant, intellectual, and novelist Romesh Chunder Dutt (1848–1909) made this connection in a pamphlet, 'Indian Famines: Their Causes and Prevention', published in 1901. Trade with Britain, he said, drained the countryside of surplus food, and made famines more likely. What was this state good for, the nationalists asked when so many lives perished in starvation and disease?

Defenders of the empire felt compelled to respond. The most influential response was the administrator John Strachey's book *India: Administration and Progress*, first published as lectures in 1888 and as a book in 1903. Strachey was the governor of an agricultural province in northern India, and later the equivalent of a finance minister in India in the 1880s. During his tenure as the head of finance, duties were reduced to encourage trade. Strachey listed the benefits of empire, such as, the growth of trade, a rule of law that rose above the inequity and diversity of Indian society, the spread of useful knowledge, and expansion in cultivation. Such sympathetic accounts still needed to explain what was going wrong in the countryside. For some administrators, the answer was the exploitative moneylender, a theory I shall discuss fully in Chapter 4.

The catalogue of benefits looked pitiful against the horrors of the holocaust. What good is law if millions of people starve? Most present-day assessments of British colonialism find in famines the clinching evidence to show what kind of rule it stood for: brutal, uncaring, and chaotic. The nationalists won. Passion was overwhelmingly on their side.

Were the facts on their side? Economic historians have the habit of looking long and hard at numbers. In the late 1970s, an American scholar Michelle McAlpin did that with the Deccan famines. This region, one of the driest agricultural zones of the world, had never been free of acute scarcities for more than 10–15 years at a stretch in the recorded history of famines in India. But famines disappeared here after 1899, McAlpin observed.

The significance of the end of famines was momentous, not just for India, for the world. It turned the population growth curve up. Between 1872 when censuses began and 1901, Deccan famines killed almost as many people as those added during two of the three decades that passed. A high death rate matched a high birth rate. After 1900, the birth rate remained high, the death rate fell because famines disappeared and because epidemic diseases were brought under control. If the unusual influenza epidemic of 1918 is excluded, people born after 1900 lived longer, and more children born after 1900 survived childhood diseases. The average life expectancy was 25 years for 1821–1871, fell to about 20 in 1871–1921 due to the unusual level of famine and influenza deaths, rising to about 35 in 1951. The Bengal Famine did not disturb that trajectory.

The British were still the rulers of India in the 40 odd years after the last of the Deccan famines when the mortality decline happened. Did colonial rule help end famines? If it did, perhaps despotic callousness of the rulers was not the reason famines had happened before? Perhaps famines happened because the state lacked the capacity to cope with disasters. The alternative explanation allows the possibility that the state slowly gained that capacity, and that famines disappeared because the regime built the means to deal with them. If the Deccan famines had happened for reasons other than the indifference, chaos or the brutality of the rule, perhaps there were other reasons at work in Bengal too?

An alternative view of famines emerged from attempts to answer these questions. Famines do not tell us much about Britain's apathy towards Indian subjects. Famines show instead that the instruments necessary to know and deal with these events evolved gradually. The years of the Deccan famines saw unusual climatic conditions caused by the El Niño Southern Oscillation phenomenon. Weather shocks of similar severity repeated after 1900 in at least four years. 'Yet the potential dangers were largely dealt with'.[3] The instruments were, a railway system that carried food quickly from low-price to high-price areas (as McAlpin noted); a statistical system to track weather and harvest conditions; knowledge of tropical diseases that killed many weakened by starvation; private charities; and a state-run relief system. The government worked to improve its ability to deal with famines. The strategy paid off.

A good illustration of such pattern of response is the same young man whose eyewitness account this chapter started with. S. Y. Padmanabhan was a mycologist, employed (in 1973, when he wrote this piece) in the Central Rice Research Institute, the last scientific research institution created by the British Indian government, in direct response to the Bengal Famine of 1943 when a part of the rice crop inexplicably failed. A more familiar example of the response is medical research at the turn of the twentieth century. The population miracle in 1899–1943 had owed to research done on some of the common killer diseases that spread quickly during and after famines, malaria, plague, cholera, and enteric diseases. The research concentrated in 1880–1900, the time span between the first and the last of the great Deccan famines.

In the same years, the technology of transporting food developed. The technology embodied in the railways came from Britain, though it had to adapt to Indian conditions. Railways were not just another item in the catalogue of 'benefits' of empire. It had a profound impact on ending famines. Current statistical research confirms McAlpin's insight that the railways caused the end of famines and delivered the gift of life to generations of Indians born after 1900.[4]

This book is about the economic legacies of British rule in India. It revisits the question, what the colonial rule was good for, and to answer it, draws on evidence-based studies done by economic historians in the last four decades. I have begun the book with the famines because it is especially hard to take a dispassionate view of the legacies of colonialism in this field. Start with famines, and you will conclude that the regime did not care about welfare. But start with the end-of-famines, and you will conclude that the regime's attitude did not matter, its capacity to cope mattered more. It is necessary to keep both the successes and the failures in view. The book suggests that the legacy of colonialism is a paradox and that any story that tells us that it did more harm than good or the other way around is one-sided.

Besides the extreme context of famines, the question—what was colonial rule good for?—turns up also in the context of markets. Between 1850 and 1930, India was engaged in a globalization process, not unlike the one it has seen since the 1990s. The difference between these two times is that much of the region was under British colonial rule during the first episode and formed of nation-states in the second. The British Indian state did not write an economic policy statement, let alone working to one. But it behaved as if it wanted openness at all costs. The result of this policy was trade with low tariffs, zero barriers to migration, an open border to investment, and smooth transmission of technologies and institutions.

After 1850, openness had political and ideological backing, and it was also favoured by British exporters, bankers, and skilled migrants all of whom wanted opportunities in the colonies. Numerous Indian merchants and bankers, especially those who quickly expanded their business beyond India, from Natal to Aden to Central Asia to East Africa to Hong Kong, held with the European businesses of the time that the British Empire gave them a good deal. Merchants who traded overland in the Indo-Gangetic Basin agreed with that view and tacitly or openly supported British India against the rebels during the Great Indian Mutiny of 1857–1858.[5]

Still, the empire *was* a despotic state. The colonialists did not consult anyone except their friends in London when they foisted globalization on to the Indians. It was their choice. Was it a good choice?

Around 1900, two intellectuals, Dadabhai Naoroji (1825–1917) and Romesh Dutt (mentioned before) wrote books claiming that it was a bad choice from the Indian point of view. Dutt said that free trade destroyed the traditional handicrafts and made Indians poorer. Naoroji said that India purchased too many services from Britain, the payment for which was a 'tribute' and a 'drain' of resources, implying that had this money stayed in India it would raise investment and economic growth. Later, these two writers were bracketed as 'nationalists', though they were not really campaigners for self-rule. Naoroji's argument became known as the drain theory of Indian poverty.

As with famines, we should take a long and hard look at the data. And when we do, the Naoroji-Dutt case does not look strong. Many artisans did suffer unemployment due to free trade. But the handicrafts revived in the twentieth century when free trade was still going strong. The drain should mean paying too much for something that India bought from Britain. Colonial India ran an export surplus, which, together with foreign investment, was used to pay for services purchased from Britain. These payments included interest on public debt, salaries, and pensions paid to government officers who had come from Britain, salaries of managers and engineers, guaranteed profits paid to railway companies, and repatriated business profits. How do we know that any of these payments involved paying too much? The answer is we do not. Naoroji shrugged off the problem by treating the entire export surplus as a waste of money. K. N. Chaudhuri rightly calls such practice 'confused' economics 'coloured by political feelings'.[6]

To some extent, monetary transactions between India and Britain reflected the fact that this was a government with two heads. Financial transactions between the two countries did not represent a British plot to bleed India; these were instead characteristic of a kind of state that European colonialism had created in the nineteenth century, a government with multiple heads. The government of India sat in both London and India, the London end minding the monetary system and the Indian end the fiscal system. Financial transfers between the two countries was a reallocation of money between branches of the same government.

Did India gain any advantage from a state with multiple heads? Of course, it did. The fact that the India Office in London managed a part of the monetary system made India creditworthy, stabilized its currency, and encouraged foreign savers to put money into railways and private enterprise in India. Current research on the history of public debt shows that stable and large colonies found it easier to borrow abroad than independent economies because the investors trusted the guarantee of the colonist powers. The British Indian army and the Royal Navy protected the empire, and the empire protected the interests of the enormous diaspora of Indian merchants and workers. Without the empire's military might, we would not get Indians doing business in Hong Kong, Aden, or Natal. The price the Indian taxpayers paid for this system was not small. The salaries of top officers were excessive; Indians were denied entry into these jobs. Surely there was overpayment. Was there drain in the net? Who can tell!

The discussion about drain focuses too much on the government, which was a tiny part of the economy. It employed two per cent of the workforce, and the top officers were one in 500 government workers. A bigger flow of funds occurred in the business sector. Businesses, we can safely assume, would not pay money for anything without assured value in return. Between 1860 and 1930, the fourth largest cotton textile mill industry and the tropical world's largest iron and steel industry emerged in India. In both cases, Indian merchants who made money in foreign trade invested their profits in the industry. The cotton merchants did not understand machines and did not know Indians who could run them. These machines and the engineers could be obtained from Manchester. Two generations later, India's most ambitious industrial venture then, Tata Steel, again relied heavily on foreign experts. The Indian mill owners were not alone in relying on foreign expertise. Many people in the nineteenth century had a stake in the free exchange of services. The medical advances that contributed to the end of famines would not occur without the open borders to scientists. Indians purchased skilled services from abroad because they needed these to run their business or their institutions.

A fair assessment of the legacy of such a state as this one should measure the *net* effect of the benefits and costs. Writings on the economic history of colonialism have not done this yet, as we see next.

Is the Paradox Explained?

As I write this book, the commercial press and popular history books have a great effect on the discussion on economic change in British India. These works make the case that colonialism inflicted profound damage on the Indian economy.[7] The authors of two of these books insist that Britain is morally bound to pay reparation to India because the damage was great. The judgemental tone, the shocking message, and perhaps the prospect of wresting money from the British taxpayer, have a powerful hold on popular imagination. Type the words 'how did the British ruin India' in Google, to find that over a million websites have answered this question, and the answer is the same every time, that the British ruined India via the drain, de-industrialization, and famine.

'In the eighteenth century', writes the author of one of the more successful narratives in this style, 'India's share of the world economy was as large as Europe's. By 1947, after two centuries of British rule, it had decreased sixfold'.[8] This was a result of Britain's 'looting' of India, which made a rich region poor. The loot began with the 'plunder' of Indian wealth by East India Company officers like Robert Clive and continued via unequal trade in the nineteenth century. The free trade policy of the empire ruined India's artisans and enabled Britain to build a world-leading textile industry. Likewise, the British Indian state paid a sum of money every year to Britain for services like interest on public debt or salaries of expatriate military officers. This drain of resources left India poorer. Though the British did introduce some instruments of modernization such as railways and the rule of law, these 'supposed "gifts" were in fact designed in Britain's interests alone'. Famines revealed how indifferent the state was to the welfare of ordinary Indians.

The media loves the sensational storyline. Liberal use of words like 'depredation', 'loot', 'rapaciousness', 'vicious', 'brutality', 'plunder', and 'extraction' adds to the drama. The forceful tone of these works is refreshing. But they offer poor-quality history. The narrative of colonial loot recycles old ideas rejected by many. It employs bad logic. And it reads the evidence in a biased manner.

There is no new discovery here. The case rests on famines, drain, and de-industrialization, which the nationalists wrote about, and which many have questioned. The analysis is simplistic. For example, the statistic that India produced 25% of world output in 1800 and 2–4% of it in 1900 does not prove that India was once rich and later became poor. It tells us nothing about India. It only tells us that industrial productivity in the West increased four to six times during this period.

There is a biased citation of scholarship and reading of the data. For example, the works cited do not deal enough with the regime's successes and therefore overstate and misread its failures. They do not ask why famines ended, why Indian businesses supported the empire until 1930, what effect openness had, or why drain is a controversial concept. These works present the nationalist paradigm as a canon, when in fact it is deeply controversial. They fail to acknowledge those who question the nationalist position as if those who stray from the true faith deserve to be treated as untouchables. They use words like drain and extraction casually as if everybody should know what these words mean. In fact, no one knows what they mean. These words cannot be exactly defined. These writings do not say in convincing detail what the record of colonial rule was, what facts we should be explaining, and ignore a tradition of scholarly research using statistical data.

Serious scholarship is not so judgemental. Most academic histories admit that the empire delivered some good outcomes and some bad outcomes. But academic writings underestimate the weight of both the good outcome and the bad ones. In the end, they offer too insipid a storyline, suggesting that everything about the economic history of colonial

India was unexciting. Why write books, then? For Dietmar Rothermund, colonial India was survival 'under conditions of low-level equilibrium', and an example of 'parasitical symbiosis .. which benefited the alien usurpers and paralysed the host'.[9] For B. R. Tomlinson, despite some signs of dynamism, India did not experience 'anything that can properly be called "development" under British rule'.[10]

This book does not share the dreary message of academic history. I believe that the regime's success was ground-breaking, and its failure had appalling consequences for Indians. And both are puzzles to be explained. Before I discuss these outcomes, it will be useful to have a brief recap of how the state came into being.

The Creation of British India

British rule in India began from territories over which the British East India Company acquired control around 1770. The rule expanded from Bengal in eastern India towards north, west, and south India via strategic alliances formed with friendly powers against hostile ones, and a series of battles to subdue the hostile powers. While fighting these battles, the British needed to raise more money and a reliable standing army. Most Indian states relied on military-cum-feudal lords for both taxation and the supply of soldiers. Such loyalty often failed. The British took a different road and raised an army of paid soldiers. This was done by reforms of the land tax system that turned the lords from military agents into landowners. In the process, the Company created a state that could collect more tax per head and operated a more powerful military machine.

Towards the end of the 1600s, the Company's local officers had set up three bases on the coast—Madras, Bombay, and Calcutta. Until 1740, Bombay, Calcutta, and Madras were small settlements of merchants and soldiers. But their role changed thereafter. In the eighteenth century, many Indian merchants and bankers fled the embattled princely states and moved into the safety of these three cities. The richest people in these towns around 1820 were Indians, with interest in shipbuilding, Indo-China trade, coastal trade, Arabian Sea trade, and overland trade.

In 1858, the Crown took over control of the Company's territory in India. At that moment, British India had three strengths that had no parallel in the region. First, the centrally controlled army had created a degree of political unification that India had never seen before. Thanks to its military might, the British could bully the independent princes to keep their own forces small and their markets and trade routes open. Second, because of this arrangement, the region was emerging as one huge integrated market. Third, the seaboard, which earlier traded a lot with Asia and Africa, now also traded with Europe, thanks to the three port cities. Indeed, these three cities were among the world's biggest hubs of maritime trade at their peak (around 1920).

The start of Crown rule coincided with Britain's Industrial Revolution, big changes in transport and communication, and the first globalization, or a growth of trade, migration, and capital investment unprecedented in scale. The Industrial Revolution created a huge demand for food and industrial material, a lot of this came from the tropical regions. The expansion of British hegemony over almost a third of the globe allowed for trade, migration, and investment to increase manifold. From 1858 until 1920, British rule in India functioned as if its main aim was to keep this exchange going, an exchange dominated by Britain and of which India was a crucial part.

What result did these changes lead to?

Net Results

Measurement must play a big role in answering the question. Economic historians have long known that, but what they publish is often published in method-heavy professional journals, get too caught up in the detail, and fail to emphasize the point. I will break with that practice and use statistics in its most basic form. In fact, only two simple charts will serve as the template for the whole book.[11]

The pair of graphs below (Fig. 1.1) divides up real national income in the early twentieth century into two parts—what the peasants earned (thin line), and what the merchants, industrialists, service workers, and bankers earned (bold line). The graph at the left tracks total income in million rupees, and the graph at the right tracks income per worker in rupees, both at 1938–1939 prices. I am going to suggest with this evidence that the economy saw a deep structural change in the colonial times.

My way of presenting national income data is different from the usual way of reading national income data. The usual way is to look at average or per capita (per person) income, note that the growth rate in per capita income was small, and then conclude that nothing happened that is worth reporting. Observing the average income leads to wrong

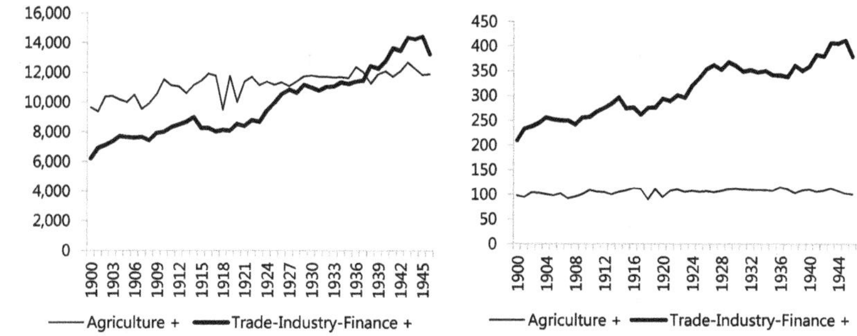

Fig. 1.1 Structural change: Business growth and agricultural stagnation. National income (million Rs., left) and income per worker (Rs. per head, right) by activity, 1938–1939 prices (*Source* S. Sivasubramonian, *National Income of India in the Twentieth Century*, New Delhi: Oxford University Press, 2000), Tables 6.2 and 2.11. The figures exclude the government, and Rural Rent

conclusions if the real story is hidden in inequality and not in the average. The average income also underestimates the productivity per worker if a growing number of working-age people stop working. I will show later that many women did stop doing paid work in these years.

I depart from another usual way of reading national incomes, which is to observe that the percentage change in *industrial* output and employment was low and conclude that since the impetus to industrialize was weak nothing much happened that is worth reporting. Rothermund, on this basis, dismisses India's business growth as 'marginal', 'retarded', confined to 'a few enclaves'.[12] This is a misreading that follows from the superstition that industrialization is the best kind of economic change. This 1970s industry fetish has now become largely obsolete. The recent economic growth in India led by the service sector has made it obsolete. My ground for rejecting the industry fetish is a little different. Colonial India was a trading economy first and foremost. Industry and finance were extensions of trade in agricultural commodities, as I show in Chapter 3. So deep was the interconnection between trade, industry, and finance that it does not make sense to distinguish these activities.

When we club business activities and contrast their record with that of agriculture, the pattern of inequality and structural change appears in sharp relief. There was good growth of one part of the economy and stagnation in another part. Business did well. The business growth curve, in fact, underestimates the true extent of business growth. Measuring income from trade is difficult, and the rule of thumb that was followed in national income studies (multiplying employment with an estimated average income) bore little relationship with the enormous rise in the physical volume of trade (see Fig. 3.1 later) and made no allowance for productivity increases in trading. While business grew, agriculture, the largest livelihood stagnated. Agriculture did expand by conversion of wasteland in the nineteenth century. When we average over business and agriculture, average national income grew at a respectable rate in the late nineteenth century. But in the interwar period, agriculture stagnated and the population rose, so that average income grew at a disastrously small rate.[13]

Part of the reason that average income growth fell was that population had started rising. The second of the two charts deals with population growth. In a region where famines had occurred frequently, famines began to become rare after 1900, resulting in a permanent fall in mortality rates (Fig. 1.2). Almost the entire natural increase in population in the last quarter of the nineteenth century was removed due to the three great famines of 1876, 1896, and 1898. But thereafter, episodes of food scarcity did not lead to mass deaths on the scale they did in the past.

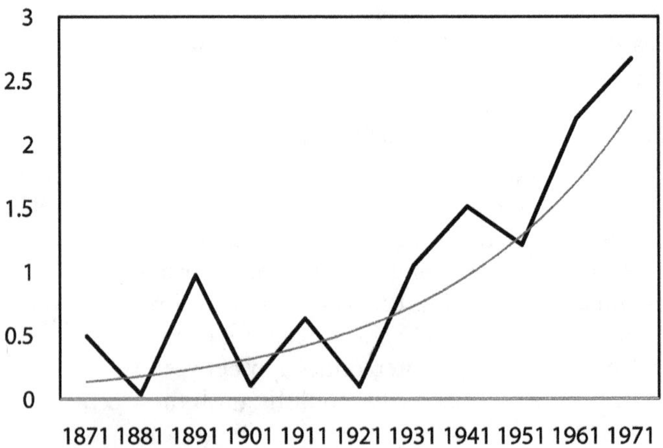

Fig. 1.2 Population transition. Average population growth rate (% per year per decade) with a trend line added (*Source* Censuses of India)

The smooth fitted line shows that the inflection occurred around 1915, and there was no significant population shock thereafter (the 1921 drop was due to the influenza epidemic, a one-off event). The Bengal Famine of 1943 does not affect that conclusion. A humanitarian disaster caused by World War II, it was not a great population shock and did not affect average longevity.

The graphs show that India scored success in business growth and mortality decline, and failure in agriculture. What had the empire to do with any of this?

The Raj's Success

The regime maintained an open economy. The productivity growth in the capitalistic activities and the mortality decline were the unintended consequences of this openness. To see that connection, first consider the three main sources of productivity growth in non-agricultural activities: trade and transport, factories, and handicrafts.

A big source of productivity gain was modern transportation, especially railways, which served overseas and overland trade. Railways encouraged trade by bringing down the costs of trade to a fraction of what it was, and the railways made its own operations more efficient with time. As John Hurd II has shown, the railways reduced the average cost of carriage of goods by over 90% compared with the pre-railway and alternative modes of transportation used in long-distance overland trade, such as bullock caravans, carts, and boats. The cargo carried by the railways increased from about three million tonnes to 120 million between 1871 and 1929. While improving the productivity of trade, the railways also improved its own productivity. Between 1865 and 1930, employment in India's railway system, then one of the largest in the world, increased from 34,000 to 790,000. In other words, cargo carried per person employed increased from 88 to 151 tonnes.[14]

Around 1920, India led the tropical world in two of the leading industries of the first Industrial Revolution, metallurgy and cotton textiles. Both gained from open borders to technology and skills. Workers in these activities gained substantially in wages and working conditions. Productivity per worker in factories was about four times that of a worker in the handicraft industries in 1900, though the gap narrowed to two-and-a-half times towards the end of the period, and anywhere between eight to ten times that of an agricultural labourer. A rise in the proportion of factory in employment, therefore, added to productivity gain on average. Employment in factories in British India increased from less than one per cent of industrial employment in 1860 to 11% in 1938.[15]

Productivity rose in the handicrafts as well. Traditional artisans like masons, carpenters, blacksmiths, and leather workers could reapply their skills to meet rising urban demand. Not everyone could do this, but many did. Masons engaged in urban construction saw a rise in wages. So did carpenters making European-style furniture or repairing tools in factories; blacksmiths making cutlery or working in forging and casting; and leather workers making new styles of footwear.

Productivity rose also in the crafts producing traditional articles. Handloom weaving of cloth was by far the largest handicraft. Between 1900 and 1930, the volume of handloom cloth production about doubled, even as the number of looms did not change. A substantial section of the handloom weaving industry in these years adapted successfully to serving urban consumers, especially, middle-class women, adopted new technology, and by hiring more wage-workers increased the average hours worked. If there was a de-industrialization, that process had run out of course by 1900, making way for a consolidation of artisanal industry thereafter. Cheap imports of raw materials like yarn and dyes and the inflow of tools and processes invented in Europe helped the Indian artisans.

Reliable national income statistics start from 1900. Many measurable indices relating to commerce, infrastructure, mining, and agriculture, confirm that the growth we observe in the twentieth century had started from at least the 1880s, possibly even before. John Strachey's claim that there was a large increase in foreign and domestic trade, due to the use of railways-posts-telegraphs, was correct. To this list, we can add factory employment, production of coal, and the real value of bank deposit. The one big area, agriculture, where growth seemed to disappear in the twentieth century had a different experience in the late 1800s. There was a rise in the cultivated area (50–60%), in the irrigated area, and occasionally real agricultural wages.

Underlying all these changes, there was a new valuation of knowledge, shared between the society and the state. Producers of goods and services were using better tools and processes than before. British India's Indian subjects lived in the shadow of an ongoing scientific-technological revolution. Members of both sets believed that transmission of useful knowledge from Britain to India could solve some of India's problems. Indian businesses who made money by trading or manufacturing understood this point perfectly. They hired skilled workers from abroad, sponsored higher and technical education, set up colleges and schools to impart western scientific knowledge, where many instructors came from abroad. The princely states built railways relying mainly on foreign expertise. The payment for these transactions Indian nationalists dismissed as the drain. They were being cynical.

Economic historians who write about how the whole world changed since the 1820s when Britain saw the beginning of industrialization, tend to divide the world into two halves, those countries that experienced what Simon Kuznets called 'modern' economic growth or growth driven by productivity gains, and those that did not. India and China are clubbed with the basket cases that did not see modern economic growth. Economic historians then ask, why did these poor countries not share in the fruits of western advances? In recent scholarship, this is known as the 'divergence' question. Figure 1.1 rejects this way of dividing the world and dismisses the divergence question as an irrelevant one. Modern economic growth happened in India too. But it did not appear with the same force across all activities. Why not? That is the question economic historians ought to be asking.

A great deal of modern enterprise was confined to the port cities. Cosmopolitanism was the port city's chief strength. Merchants in these cities knew the overseas markets and countries intimately, sometimes relocated business to other parts of the empire, and acquired the purchasing power to buy technologies, skills, and knowledge from Britain. More skilled people and more services migrated to these cities.

The people whom trade made rich had access to state-of-the-art knowledge and technology of their times. In turn, they took education and technology extremely seriously. The more globally exposed the set, the more aware the rich were of the importance of investing in education, whether for their own children or for their community or the society at large. Some of the coastal trading groups (like the Parsis) had the highest levels of education and female literacy around 1900, over 50% when the average literacy level was below ten per cent. Without the rich Indian merchants of nineteenth-century selling cotton or indigo, Indians would not get the Presidency College of Calcutta or the Elphinstone College of Bombay, still two of the best colleges in the country.

At independence in 1947, the port cities were homes to some of the best schools, colleges, hospitals, universities, banks, insurance companies, charities, and learned societies available outside the western world, much of it built with capitalist profits; hired foreigners often ran them.

Openness, therefore, was much more than trading, it was also a transaction in science, technology, organizational and institutional ideas. Public health was one area where such transactions produced results. The upturn in population trend had owed to the end of famines. But that was only one factor. The others were improvements in public health and reduction in child mortality. The medical bureaucracy was too small to respond effectively to famines and epidemics, but it was filled with part-time scientists who conducted research on tropical diseases, nutrition, hygiene, the social conditions that made infections spread quickly, and the ecological setting that made malaria destructive. The staff of this service and the doctors outside it observed the great difference in the effectiveness of public health measures between Britain and India and worried about how to bridge the gap. The result was that by 1920, some of the biggest sources of mass death and debility in the region had become considerably weaker than these were in the nineteenth century. Infant mortality rates fell from 200 in 1901 to 116 in 1951. Life expectancy about doubled in these 50 years.

Even the harshest critics of the empire acknowledged some of the benefits of globalization. But then, the Deccan famines struck while the globalization was in full swing. Most peasants barely managed to earn a subsistence. Vast areas in central India covered in forests and shrubs were as badly connected to the trading world as ever. Why did so much of the society fail to benefit from the fruits of the colonial economy?

The Raj's Failure

The immediate cause of poverty and stagnation in the countryside was low land yield. In 1927, the Royal Commission on Agriculture in India confirmed a view among scientists and economists that land yields had remained stagnant through expansion in cultivation, and that Indian yields were significantly smaller than yields of similar crops in East Asia, North Africa, Europe, and North America. In the 1960s, when George Blyn reworked agricultural production and yield data, confirmation of diminishing returns was found from major crops grown in much of India, especially in Eastern India. The statistician Moni Mukherjee's calculation of total factor productivity growth for 1900–1946 showed that the contribution of yield to agricultural income growth was negligible.[16]

Many officers understood what was wrong with the countryside, that in this tropical land, water was the scarcest resource, scarcer even than land, and that most people had too little good land and too little assured supply of water. Although India exported a lot of agricultural goods, agricultural productivity was low throughout because the major part of the land is arid or semi-arid, where monsoon rains permitted growing one main seasonal crop but acute water scarcity in the rest of the year prohibited intensive and multiple cropping. Small peasants and labourers in the dryland and upland areas and the overpopulated eastern Gangetic Basin stayed poor even as agricultural production increased.

Some officers engaged with agriculture, especially the engineers and scientists believed that they knew what the solution to the problem was, irrigation. Neither the geography nor the capacity of the state made taking that step easy. The state could follow that recipe to a limited extent. It had limited financial capacity. Transforming tropical agriculture required large-scale investment in water supply systems, often at a serious environmental cost. And even with such investment, the semi-arid areas might not get enough water.

Not surprisingly, the average wage was low and stagnant. The agricultural labour market was not in complete inertia. The force of tradition weakened. Rural labourers who worked under conventional bondage fell in numbers, and migration to new land frontiers increased. Agricultural wages became more negotiable from before. But agricultural real wages were almost constant, thanks to stagnant productivity of the land.

My account, then, is not a happy one. It rejects the nationalist myth that colonial rule was evil. But it does not celebrate colonialism in the style of Strachey. By relying on the nineteenth-century globalization and Britain's scientific advances, the British rulers could indirectly foster business growth and end famines. The state was, however, too weak an agent to transform a resource-poor countryside. Where the state was needed, it was not there. In this way, the regime deepened inequality. It deepened inequality in another way.

My version of history is closer to the true spirit of Indian nationalism. The Naoroji-Dutt version of nationalism is unreliable, being 'coloured by political feelings'. It deflects attention away from India's own structural problems. Nationalism is not about bashing the enemies of the nation but acquiring the ability to think of the nation as a collection of equal citizens. Key thinkers in the colonial times—M. K. Gandhi (1869–1948), Rabindranath Tagore (1861–1941), B. R. Ambedkar (1891–1956)—understood this and knew that creating an equal nation would be a challenging task for most Indians. India's problem was a society ridden by inequalities between castes and gender. Some publicists (like the leader of the lower castes Ambedkar) believed that the British, being outsiders to the Hindu society, should be welcomed as they could break the power of caste.

Any modernizing drive largely bypassed those already exploited. Openness favoured capital-owning communities more than the labouring ones. Among the latter, low social status and limited earning power remained concentrated. There was probably a lot more mobility among the lower castes than ever before in history, but not enough to change the distribution of economic and political power.

What was true of caste was true also of women. Industrial productivity improved because work moved to the factories. But factories did not want women. For much of the twentieth century, the censuses show that the proportion of women among industrial workers fell. Further, the end of famine and rising longevity increased women's burden at home. More surviving births meant that women stayed longer at home to mind children.

In 1927, an American journalist Katherine Mayo published a book called *Mother India*, highlighting appalling gender inequality and abuse that would then be accepted as conventional by many Indians. Mayo subjected the generic Indian man, his beliefs and his religion to vitriol. But statistics on marriage, jobs, health status showed that she had a case. Ten years later, a more balanced book by an academic (Vera Anstey, *Economic Development of India*) used the data to show how women got a raw deal during India's modernization.

The state failed to commit enough money or energy to improve society. Its record on investment in schools was poor, gender disparity was not even recognized as a goal. I confess that I do not believe that a state can do social reform without the society helping it. By social reform, we mean equality of opportunity and equality in society. Indian society was not ready to accept either in the British colonial times. Divisions and hierarchy were too entrenched in the mindset for that.

These very divisions and hierarchy were weaker in the port cities. Cities had more schools, hospitals, courts of law within easy access of the poor. More women went to school here, worked for wages, joined public life, and occasionally managed family firms. Caste oppression was less onerous in the mill neighbourhood. Bombay's business world in the 1800s saw partnerships between Hindus, Muslims, Europeans, and Parsis—a collaboration that would be unthinkable anywhere else in India in that time. Perhaps the cosmopolitanism of the cities made them less oppressive spaces. Perhaps in the port cities, there was more of the sentiment that Deirdre McCloskey calls 'bourgeois virtue'.[17] Or, as the explorer Richard Burton said of Malabar merchants in 1853, 'affluence softened them'. But the society at large did not believe in bourgeois virtue. Neither cosmopolitanism nor affluence had softened it. And colonial rule did not commit itself seriously to the cause either.

A similar failure occurred in public health. The fruits of the development in epidemiology and public health concentrated in the cities. Health measures in the villages were poor. Sanitation, campaign for hygiene, the supply of clean water, were among measures that had brought about a dramatic improvement in life expectancy in Britain in the same decades that life expectancy fell in India (1871–1921). The contrast was well-known to health officers in India and Britain, but the government did not commit money to make India more like Britain.[18] Businesses used the new knowledge much better when they built hospitals. Its reach was limited to the port cities.

The Story in a Nutshell and How It Relates to World History

How, then, did colonialism change India's economy? Here is a summary of the argument of the book. I have shown that the nationalist claim that colonialism ruined India's economy fails the test of Figs. 1.1 and 1.2. By committing itself to openness, the British Empire in India enabled trade and technology transfer on a scale the region would not have seen otherwise. The resultant India–Britain exchange helped businesses grow and ended famines. But colonialism and globalization left the countryside almost untouched and worsened inequality between men and women, and between capital and labour. The state could, in theory, invest in the countryside and mitigate inequality. It was a formidable challenge, one that the state did not take on.

Let me now for a moment wear my academic's hat and discuss the intellectual context of this argument. I build on a perspective about colonialism that others have used. But the book uses it to a fuller extent than others have done.

Economic historians of the world read the significance of European colonialism by following one of two approaches. One of these emphasizes European intentions and capacities to rule and infers the pattern of economic change in countries like India from these intentions and capacities. In the 1970s, Marxist intellectuals like André Gunder Frank, Samir Amin, and Immanuel Wallerstein saw colonialism as a machine that extracted value from the third world and transferred it to Europe. Some Marxists said that the British colonialists underdeveloped India by empowering the landlords.[19] More recently, institutional economic history popular in North America claims that, whereas the rule of law created economic prosperity in Europe, the Europeans did not extend the same favour to countries like India, creating instead exploitative states.

The second perspective starts from the premise that European rule was a weaker and a more limited form of rule than these models of predatory colonialism suggest. This approach would tell us that local conditions rather than European intentions or capacities had a bigger effect on the pattern of economic change to follow. These local conditions included a robust business heritage and resource-poor agriculture. Colonialism strengthened the former, failed to change the latter, and in effect increased inequality.

I follow the second approach. The former approach is not persuasive for several reasons. First, it is Europe-centred. Second, the intention of the state is assumed rather than proven. Third, it overstates the role of the state. A recent scholarship measuring the financial capacity of colonial states has shown that these states were so small and so weak that their power to do either good or bad was extremely limited.[20] Take rule of law, for example. The British in India made many excellent laws but had little money to spend on the system of justice. For the poor Indians going to court was expensive. What good was a rule of law, then? Fourth, the concept of an exploitative state tends to be unclear on what exploitation means. In the 1970s Marxist canon, exploitation was equated with almost any trade, which makes little sense.

The second approach pays more attention to India's own situation than to British intentions in reading the long-term pattern of economic change. Other scholars have applied the second approach before me. In an exploratory paper, Christopher Bayly said that colonialism offered Indian merchants an opportunity to strengthen their capability by doing business in the world economy and that they invested the profits in education and healthcare.[21] Bayly was right. But we need to take this thesis to its logical conclusion and show also those whom this process did not benefit. The book does that.

Conclusion

The short summary of the argument in the previous section is enough to set out the six questions the next six chapters will answer. How did globalization and colonialism unfold (Chapter 2)? Why were these forces good for business (Chapter 3)? Why did the peasants produce more and yet stay poor (Chapter 4)? Why was the government unable to spend more money (Chapter 5)? Why did famines end (Chapter 6)? What about the princely states? Did they experience a different pattern of growth (Chapter 7)?

Finally, I claim that the narrative has a contemporary relevance for emerging economies, where again globalization has unleashed extraordinary levels of capitalistic energy while leaving many livelihoods poor, stagnant, and discontented. Chapter 8 comments on the paradox of emergence, which connects the two globalization in India a century apart.

First, let us see how this state came into being.

Notes

1. The Raj is a common and handy reference to the British Empire in India, especially outside India. The word derives from the Sanskrit word *rajya*, meaning state or government. Princely states and landlord estates in northern India often used it to refer to themselves.
2. Jon Wilson, *India Conquered*, London: Simon and Schuster, 2016.
3. Tim Dyson, *Population History of India*, Oxford: Clarendon Press, 2018, 158.
4. Robin Burgess and Dave Donaldson, 'Can Openness Mitigate the Effects of Weather Shocks? Evidence from India's Famine Era,' *American Economic Review*, 100(2), 2010, 449–453.
5. Tirthankar Roy, 'The Mutiny and the Merchants,' *The Historical Journal*, 59(2), 2016, 393–416.
6. K.N. Chaudhuri, 'India's International Economy in the Nineteenth Century: A Historical Survey,' in G. Balachandran, ed., *India and the World Economy*, Delhi: Oxford University Press, 2003, 46–69.

7. Shashi Tharoor, *Inglorious Empire: What the British Did to India*, London: C. Hurst, 2017; Wilson, *India Conquered*; Utsa Patnaik, 'Profit Inflation, Keynes, and the Holocaust in Bengal, 1943–44,' *Economic and Political Weekly*, 53(42), 2018, 33–43; and Utsa and Prabhat Patnaik, *A Theory of Imperialism*, New York: Columbia University Press, 2018. Read also review of Tharoor's book in the *Cambridge Review of International Affairs*, 31(1), 2018, 134–138.
8. Blurb of Tharoor, *Inglorious Empire*.
9. Dietmar Rothermund, *An Economic History of India*, London and New York: Routledge, 2nd ed., 2002, vii.
10. B.R. Tomlinson, *The Economy of Modern India: From 1860 to the Twenty-First Century*, Cambridge: Cambridge University Press, 2nd ed., 2013, 9, refers to a distinction economists make between growth and development, the former being a measurable but a limited index of welfare, and the latter a better index of welfare, but poorly measurable.
11. Throughout this book, I will make statements, cite works, and cite data that are not fully referenced. More detailed discussion can be found in my *The Economic History of India 1857–1947*, Delhi: Oxford University Press, 2011.
12. *Economic History of India*, 59, 62.
13. I draw on the work of Moni Mukherjee, Alan Heston, and S. Sivasubramonian, three economists-statisticians who produced the standard dataset on India's national income.
14. For a fuller analysis, see Dan Bogart and Latika Chaudhary, 'Engines of Growth: The Productivity Advance of Indian Railways, 1874–1912,' *Journal of Economic History*, 73(4), 2013, 339–370.
15. The extent of productivity growth was smaller than the average for the Western world in the nineteenth century. This is a well-known difference between Asia and Europe, and attributed to the fact that the Asian pathway was more 'labour-intensive,' see Gareth Austin and Kaoru Sugihara, eds., *Labour-Intensive Industrialization in Global History*, Abingdon and New York: Routledge, 2012.
16. George Blyn, *Agricultural Trends in India, 1891–1947: Output, Availability, and Productivity*, Philadelphia: University of Pennsylvania Press, 1966; Mukherjee, 'Sources of Growth of the Indian Economy,' *Sankhya*, Series B, 35(2), 1973, 133–140.
17. Deirdre McCloskey, *The Bourgeois Virtues: Ethics for an Age of Commerce*, Chicago: University of Chicago Press, 2006.
18. Sheldon Watts, *Disease and Medicine in World History*, New York and London: Routledge, 2008.
19. Samir Amin, 'India: A Great Power?' *Monthly Review*, 56(9), 2005, 1–13.

20. See discussion in Tirthankar Roy, 'State Capacity and the Economic History of Colonial India,' *Australian Economic History Review*, 2018, https://onlinelibrary.wiley.com/doi/epdf/10.1111/aehr.12166, accessed on 25 October 2018.
21. C.A. Bayly, *Indigenous and Colonial Origins of Comparative Economic Development: The Case of Colonial India and Africa*, Washington, DC: World Bank Policy Research Working Paper 4474, 2008.

Further Reading

B.R. Tomlinson, *The Economy of Modern India*, Cambridge: Cambridge University Press, 2013.

Dietmar Rothermund, *Economic History of India*, London: Routledge, 2003.

Tirthankar Roy, *The Economic History of India 1858–1947*, Delhi: Oxford University Press, 2011.

CHAPTER 2

The Making of British India

Abstract A new economic world took shape in India in the 1800s. It was new in that a pattern of trade emerged that did not exist before. In the 1700s, Indians exported textiles. In the 1800s, Indians exported agricultural commodities. The emergence of the new trading order owed to two things. A powerful state ruled over both the agricultural hinterland and the seaboard. And the state was interested in overseas trade. This state was the British Empire in South Asia. The transformation led to gains for some and losses for others. The chapter describes the emergence of the new model of capitalism, its consequences, and shows why politics was so important to its emergence.

Keywords Mughal Empire · East India Company · Indian Ocean · India–China trade · Indian Mutiny

A new economic world took shape in the 1800s? How was it new?

The most significant feature of the economic world to emerge in India in the 1800s was a new pattern of trade. In the 1700s, Indians exported textiles. In the next century, Indians exported agricultural commodities. This shift was partly an outcome of the Industrial Revolution. But its beginnings in India dated before the rise of machines and had owed to two things. The same state ruled the agricultural hinterland and the seaboard. And that state was interested in overseas trade. The Mughal

© The Author(s) 2019

T. Roy, *How British Rule Changed India's Economy*,
Palgrave Studies in Economic History,
https://doi.org/10.1007/978-3-030-17708-9_2

Empire did not fulfil both these conditions. It ruled the hinterland but had weak authority on the seaboard, and was not overly keen on trade. The British Empire met these conditions.

The first process, expansion of power, was completed between 1760 and 1820. It was led by foreign merchants. These merchants enhanced their power by making alliances with Indian merchants and by expanding their military dominance over their rivals. The linking of the land and the sea—agriculture and trade—was the new state's unique legacy.

Why did it happen? What was the baseline from which it happened?

The Economy of the Inland

The Indian subcontinent has five major geographical regions: the mountains and foothills, the western desert and savannah, the floodplains of the two great Himalayan river systems (the Ganges and the Indus) or the Indo-Gangetic Basin, the peninsular or Deccan uplands, and the seaboard (see Map 2.1). At the beginning of the eighteenth century, the Himalayan foothills had been largely forested, and the desert and the savannah sustained only pastoralist groups. The history of the rise and fall of states usually concern the three other regions, the Indo-Gangetic Basin, the Deccan Plateau, and the seaboard.

Owing to fertile alluvial soil, access to the waters of the perennial Himalayan rivers, flat terrain and easier transportation, the Indo-Gangetic Basin gave rise to imperial states that lived on land tax. Power attracted wealth so that these zones had richer cities and a lot of trade. By contrast, the Deccan plateau and the central uplands were agriculturally poorer, grew locally consumed millets, participated in trade to a lesser extent, and were exposed to the threat of famines. It did have segments of rich black soil that sustained prosperous communities, but in general, the plateau was water-scarce, resource-poor, and less urban.

The seaboard was always engaged in maritime trade and drew its livelihood from it. Parts of this zone—such as the western Bengal delta, Krishna-Godavari delta, coastal Gujarat, and Malabar—were heavily involved in maritime trade. By and large, these areas were ruled by smaller states and had long received foreign settlers. The power of the Mughal Empire (1526 to about 1740) was weak in the seaboard. It was not deeply interested in maritime trade nor had naval power. But the autonomy of the seaboard states was not always backed up by military

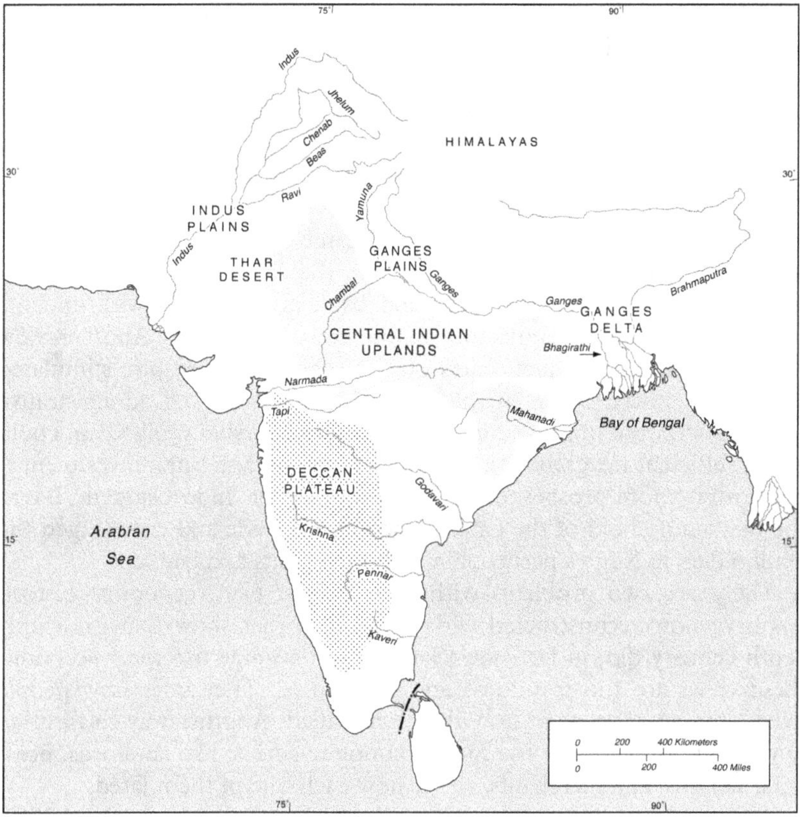

Map 2.1 Geographical zones. The map also shows major railway routes connecting the interior with the port cities from around 1880

might either, leaving them vulnerable to conquest. In one such zone, in lower Bengal delta, European colonization began in the middle of the eighteenth century.

Well before that time, and shortly after the death of the emperor Aurangzeb (1707), the Mughal Empire that had ruled over the floodplains since 1526 started breaking up. The Mughal Empire broke up for many reasons, including fiscal crisis and constant warfare.[1] Its attempt to capture the Deccan Plateau failed, among other reasons, because the Mughal army consisting of a large cavalry was not suited for battles in the dry and hilly terrains of the south. In Bengal, Hyderabad, and Awadh, former provincial governors established independent rules. In Deccan, eastern Rajasthan, and north-western India, landlords and warlords rebelled. Several new states emerged from this turmoil. Militarily the most powerful was the dominion of the Marathas ruled by several clans.

Battles between rivals and alliances became common. Did the violence affect economic conditions? In one view, the collapse of the empire led to economic collapse. Merchants and bankers connected with imperial finance and luxury manufacture in the towns suffered.[2] Another view holds that the rise of new states on the ashes of the empire stimulated economic activity. Some of the new states used the old administrative order intact, even improved it. Bengal, under Murshid Quli Khan, could devise 'efficient tax gathering procedures', encourage 'rural investments', and foster 'more prosperous agriculture'.[3] In the Indo-Gangetic Basin, the weakening hold of the empire encouraged trade and encouraged the landholders to forge a partnership with merchants and bankers.

There are two problems with these views. First, economic historians have now reconstructed fairly good data that show that the eighteenth century did, in fact, see a large fall in average income.[4] Secondly, these views are too top-down and speculative. They infer how people lived from an account of how they were ruled. Another way to form an impression is to look at the major economic actors, like landlords, peasants, artisans, and merchants, to see how each one of them fared.

The land was the source of livelihood and revenue in the 1700s. There were several types of interest and right relating to land. In northern India, the peasants had a right to cultivate land, and village landlords, often known as zamindars, had a right to collect taxes from the peasants and send a part of the collection to the treasury. Above them were military tenure-holders like the jagirdars, who were entitled to use the revenues of a large estate to maintain soldiers against the promise to fight battles for the state. They were not cultivators of land. None of these rights could be sold easily, if at all. Jagirdari was an assignment and not ownership. The assignment was not hereditary. Zamindari and peasant rights were not hereditary either. Selling land was not easy also because no one party could exclude the other from controlling land.

Still, as the power of the centre started to weaken, the right to collect tax began to be sold more often. The successor states had limited administrative and financial resources. Anyone promising to collect the tax and send a part of it to the treasury could join an auction of such rights and take out a contract. As wars became more frequent in the eighteenth century, auctions of revenue rights became more frequent too. Merchants and bankers became tax contractors or revenue farmers. Was this good news or bad for the militaristic landlords? We cannot say for sure. Many of them lost money or privilege due to warfare, but the states also depended on them more than ever.

Did peasants become better off as a result of this change? Almost certainly they did not, for tax rates were high before and remained high during the transition of power. In Mughal India, the common tax share was between one-third and one-fourth of the gross produce. Among the Marathas and in south India, rates like 50% of gross produce off irrigated land, and one-third from dry land, were usual. Actual collection from the peasant was less than the stated rate. The revenue system had a history of remissions and rescheduling in times of stress. Still, there is no sign that the rates came down. Since land yield was not high, the burden of taxation on the cultivators was a heavy one. But if the peasants did not gain, there is no sign that they suffered a serious loss either. The more likely scenario is that nothing much happened either way.

The countryside also had a large handicraft industry making basic textiles, pottery, agricultural implements, sugar, leather, and oil. Rural industry was widely dispersed, but its consumption, technology, and organization were simple everywhere. Family units produced these goods and worked with locally fabricated tools for the consumption of villagers. The exceptions were a few odd products, such as raw silk, salt, saltpetre, and indigo, that were produced in the villages by part-time peasants, and traded widely. Because peasants were poor, and their conditions did not change, there was little change in the conditions of rural artisans.

It was a different scenario with industries like silk and those in the cities. In Mughal north India, the revenue delivered to central treasury not only maintained public administration but also sustained the consumption of those connected with the state. Such people were on average wealthy and their shopping habits encouraged high-quality crafts like fine textiles, carpets and shawls, decorative metal-ware and pottery, wood and ivory carving, arms and musical instruments. Trade in these goods was well developed. The collapse of the Mughal Empire was bad news for these crafts. Skilled urban crafts earlier concentrated in a few cities in the Indo-Gangetic Basin such as Lahore, Agra, Delhi, and Multan, now moved towards new seats of power such as Benares, Farrukhabad, Lucknow, Moradabad, Jhansi, Gwalior, Bijapur, Ahmadnagar, Aurangabad, Warangal, and Madurai. It is likely that a lot of the skills, customers, and capital were lost during these movements.

Like these handicrafts, the north Indian cities were home to bankers, who funded grain trade, converted grain tax to cash, changed money, and lent money to zamindars and jagirdars. Throughout the eighteenth century, there were reports of traders and bankers shifting the base of their operations from northern India towards the successor states, and eventually the British-held port cities. The two best-documented movements were those of the north Indian Khatris towards Bengal, and the Marwari moneylenders of western India first to the successor states, and then to Calcutta. Once again, these movements could not have happened without some costs and disruptions.

There were also many merchants engaged in overland trade like grain and raw silk. In 1700, the rivers the Ganges and the Indus were the main arteries for domestic trade in bulk commodities in north India. These two routes met in the Punjab, where caravans that crossed the Himalayas to connect India with Afghanistan, Iran, and Central Asia, also joined. Apart from grain, the overland traders carried salt, cloth, spices, and horses. In the Deccan peninsula, where neither navigable rivers nor wheeled traffic could penetrate far into the interior, the main mode of overland carriage of goods was the pack bullock. Bullock trains of enormous size connected northern India with southern India and connected the coasts with the capital cities in the Deccan. Coast-to-coast shipping conducted by maritime communities supplemented the overland traffic. During the eighteenth century, a part of the network started serving the textile export trade that flourished in the coastal areas. But overland trade in grain and craft goods suffered decline.

As this description suggests, the countryside saw little change during the collapse of the Mughal Empire. But businesses were affected. The successor states provided them with at best a temporary home. In the second half of the eighteenth century, constant warfare had exhausted their fiscal capacity. Merchants and bankers were squeezed harder and often fled conflict zones to the greater safety of the British ports.

For some time, the seaboard was gaining in wealth and power.

The Rise of the Seaboard

India had long been a major link in the maritime trade between Asia and Europe. A coastline 4600 miles long, easy access from both west and east Asia, a rich tradition of cloth making, a developed shipbuilding industry, and strong mercantile tradition, consolidated India's position in the Indian Ocean.

The merchant marine came in several types. The most important ones were in Gujarat, Malabar (north Kerala), Coromandel, and Bengal. The Arabian Sea trade between Gujarat and Malabar at the Indian end and the Persian Gulf and Red Sea ports at the West Asia end was of great antiquity. Shipbuilding was an established industry in both these regions. The best timber for ships came from the Western Ghats in Kerala. Indian ships called on the ports of the Red Sea and the Persian Gulf. The market of the *hajj*, wherein caravan trade from a large area converged, was one of the principal conduits through which Indian goods, chiefly textiles and spices, found their way to European markets. In the East, Javanese shipping carried Indian textiles to the Spice Islands in eastern Indonesia in exchange for spices. The linking of sea routes and land routes, or the port-cities with the interior, was weak. Most states and empires did little to create and sustain port towns. These were rather the creation of the Indian Ocean.

The first European traders to try to control the Indian Ocean trade were the Portuguese in the 1500s. They were not too successful in this enterprise. By 1620, the entry of the Dutch and the English in this field checked Portuguese naval power. The formation of the English East India Company in 1600 (from 1708, formally, United Company of Merchants of England trading to the East Indies) under a royal charter, and the merger of several firms trading in the East Indies into the Dutch East India Company (Vereenigde Oost-Indische Compagnie or VOC) in 1602, started a new era in trade. Unlike the Portuguese, who had a reputation for bullying local merchants, the Dutch and the English did business through diplomacy and alliances with local merchants. All Europeans in the 1600s wanted to buy spices from the Indonesian archipelago and found Indian cotton textiles a convenient means of payment (Fig. 2.1).

In the late-1600s, however, Europe was a bigger market for Indian cotton textiles than was Asia. Indian cotton textiles defined fashions in clothing in British markets then. Textile exports to Europe came in

Fig. 2.1 Tombs of early English settlers in Surat. A nineteenth-century photograph showing ruins of the graveyard of European traders who came to Surat from the seventeenth century and died in the city, the main port on the western coast. European settlement in this port (as in Masulipatnam on the Coromandel coast and Cochin in the deep south, which are the homes to Dutch graveyards) was small in scale, but of long duration (© DeGolyer Library, Southern Methodist University, William Johnson Photographs of Western India)

five main types: muslins (cloths made of fine cotton yarn), fine calicoes (cloths made of medium-to-fine yarn), ordinary cotton calicoes (cloths made of coarse-medium yarn), silk cloths, and silk-cotton mixed fabrics. The term 'calico' referred to a piece of plain-weave cotton fabric, bleached or unbleached. Calico derived its name from Calicut on the Kerala coast, from where the first consignments of Indian textiles went to Europe. A part of the calico exports consisted of 'chintz', painted or printed cloth. Indian dyers were deft users of organic colouring agents and expert at fixing dyes on cotton cloth (mordanting).

The brightly coloured fabrics with Indian patterns generated so much interest in Europe that manufacturers in England and France began imitating them.

The trade depended on a plentiful supply of precious metals from Spanish America. Silver came from the Bolivian mines into the Spanish imperial fiscal system. Europeans purchased silver in Spanish ports and shipped it to India and China to pay for cotton and silk cloth. The goods they had to offer in exchange did not generate much interest in India.

By the end of the eighteenth century, Europeans dominated the routes and the markets for Indian goods. Indian shipping was not a small-scale enterprise. At its peak, the Gujarati merchant marine based in Surat consisted of about 100 vessels of 200–400 tonnes each. Many owners of ocean-going ships were politically powerful people. Still, Indian ship-owning merchants never became dominant players in trans-continental trade.

There were several factors behind European domination of world sea-borne trade. Naval superiority, thanks to a partnership between the parent state and the merchants, was one of these. Their settlements in Asia were backed by strong fleets, which not only kept the sea routes open but also kept bullying by the inland powers in check. By contrast, Indian seagoing merchants were rarely backed by their states and were sometimes exploited by them. There were also differences in technology and business organization. Although Indian ships charged lower freight rates, European ships were on average bigger, sturdier, and better defended. The structure of the ships enabled carriage of bigger cargo and more guns on board. European trade was organized around joint-stock companies, whereas Indian businesses developed around families or individuals. The stability of such a firm was too dependent on the resources and talents available in the family.

None of these 'advantages' made a British Empire in India inevitable.

The Rise of the Company State

The British East India Company (1600–1878?) was a business firm with unusual features. In England, it was politically influential, with enough clout to seek the help of the Royal Navy to protect its overseas interests. In India, it was managed by employees who commanded arms, and took independent decisions, sometimes defying the orders of their bosses in London. They needed to be armed and independent, because doing business in the

Indian Ocean led to conflict with other European traders, and occasionally with the locals. Dealing with the private traders who encroached on the Crown monopoly that the Company had, also needed political skills. The London shareholders of the firm could not play these games.

Since its foundation in 1600, therefore, the Company had built ports, docks, warehouses, and overseas settlements. Of the three major ports in India, Calcutta located in Bengal was rapidly growing in population in the 1740s, thanks to the migration of wealthy Bengali merchants from the western borders of the state where the Maratha forces stationed in central India harassed them.

Between 1740 and 1770, as the Mughal Empire collapsed and the states that succeeded it fought with each other to gain power, the Company's local officers became more ambitious. Whether to protect trade or from opportunism, they joined politics, palace intrigues, and local battles. At the same time, rivalries with the French East India Company broke out in the wake of the War of the Austrian Succession (1740–1748) and the Seven Years War (1754–1763). The rivals joined opposite camps in a power struggle in Carnatic, a small kingdom near British Madras and French Pondicherry. In Bengal, the Company ran into a dispute with the local ruler (Nawab) and allied with Indian merchants and bankers to overthrow the regime. After initial reverses against the French in the south and the Nawab of Bengal in the east, the Company became the ruler of Bengal (1757–1765) and a de facto ruler of the Carnatic (1760).

The next major acquisitions occurred in the south. The Nizams of Hyderabad were Mughal governors who established a virtually independent rule by 1730. Having suffered Maratha raids, the Nizam formed an alliance with the French. When the French became friendly with the two rival powers Mysore and Maratha, the ruler Nizam Ali Khan allied with the English (1766), handing over the 'Northern Circars', a large chunk of coastal Coromandel, to the Company against the promise of protection. In 1803, districts in the west and south of the state, including the fertile Raichur Doab, were also handed over.[5] In 1761, the main Maratha army lost a battle to the Afghans during a contest for control over northern India (the Third Battle of Panipat). After the Third Anglo-Maratha wars of 1818, the Company was the main political and military power of India.

Two modes of expansion, thus, set the pattern. The Company could coerce weak but independent states into delivering land, and it could take sides in local rivalries and gain from military victories. Between 1775 and 1818, the Rohilla Afghans, the Marathas, and Mysore had to give up lands to the British. The Sikh wars in 1846 delivered Punjab to

British control. These conflicts worried Indian princes, which turned into a panic in 1848–1856, when the British asserted the right to annex a princely state if the ruling prince was judged to be governing badly, and worse if he died without a male heir ('the doctrine of lapse'). The acquisition of Awadh (1856) followed in this way, though Awadh had been effectively colonized from long before.

By 1856, the map of British India was set. Sixty per cent of the land area and a somewhat higher percentage of the population belonged in the British ruled territory (see Map 2.2). The British controlled the coastline, possessed all important ports, and the coastal trade routes.

Map 2.2 British India and the princely states (shaded)

The remaining 40% of the area was governed by several hundred large and small kingdoms, the princely states (Chapter 7). With some of these states, the British had drawn up non-aggression treaties. The others were too small to matter, or so the British rulers thought.

Why Did Trade Lead to an Empire?

No doubt the Company was a semi-political entity from the start. But having power and using power to create a rule are different things. Why, then, did trade lead to an empire? One answer to the question is that the Company was a firm with two personalities. The shareholders in London were merchants and bankers who did not want wars and did not understand India. The branches were managed by traders, soldiers, and sailors, men who came from a different class of British society, and who were closer to those Indians on whom the firm's activities depended. They understood local politics and took interest in it. The disintegration of the Mughal Empire and warfare in Europe affected these people more than the London shareholders. The empire emerged from the limited ability of the directors to stop their employees from joining local politics.[6]

This explanation stresses the political angle too much. There was also an economic angle. In its trading operations, the Company faced problems of contract enforcement all the time. The trade that the outstation officers managed could not do without the help of many Indian bankers, brokers, agents, transporters, and wage-workers. Contracts made with these people broke down often, and when they did, the Company had little help from local kings and courts of law. At a time when these kings were even weaker than before, any trader would wish to take law in own hand.[7]

Besides politics and economics, there was a military angle to the emergence of the empire. The empire emerged from battles. The Company was a strong power in the seas. But the battles that led to its rule in India were fought on land. The military success of the Company had owed to a standing army, whereas the rivals relied on armies supplied by feudal lords. While fighting wars, Indian kings gave away more taxation rights to these warlords, which weakened the kings. The warlords had their own fish to fry and were not always loyal. Thanks to the standing army, the Company subdued the warlords, which enhanced their power as a state. Further, after the Parliament started to share the rule of India (1784, see below), its Indian partners saw the Company as a more credible ally, leading to stable alliances.[8]

Ruling and governing are different things. How did governing evolve?

Becoming a Government

Company's empire in India raised a problem for the British state. Who was the real ruler of the Indian territories, the king, the Parliament, or a business firm? Between 1757 and 1772, the enormous land that the Company had control over was ruled by a self-serving gang rather than a state. The huge personal wealth of the ringleaders made them unpopular in Britain. In these years, the land revenue of Bengal was used to finance exports. In effect, the poor Bengali peasant subsidized the rich London merchant. This was a swindle, though its scale was not large (Chapter 5). But the swindle induced the Parliament to act. In 1784, Parliament created the body (Board of Control) that would establish its oversight of British rule in India.

That transition enabled deeper institutional reform. The land was of utmost importance. The Mughals had been an agrarian empire, a state that depended on land taxes. The British at first were a maritime empire or a state that emerged from trade and funded its military enterprise by commercial profit. But as the Company acquired more regions, it needed to change itself from a maritime into an agrarian state. It needed to raise more money from the conventional sources and use it to create a stronger military machine.

Their success in doing this was significant. In Bengal, revenue per square mile increased from Rs. 236 in 1763, to 520 in 1817, and further to 724 in 1853. The average price of rice in Eastern India did not rise in this time span, so this was a trebling of revenue per mile in real terms. Besides land, the government was determined to make trade pay more. Salt, for example, was made to yield an income through an inland duty, direct profits where the government monopolized procurement, and a customs duty on imports. Similarly, opium trade was taxed.

The biggest break occurred in land tax. The Company brought land taxation under closer control, and reformed land rights. The earlier system was to have two interests in every plot of land, that of the cultivator and that of the tax collector or zamindar. This entanglement of rights created two problems. First, it left the tax-collecting landlord armed and dangerous. A zamindar needed soldiers to coerce the tax-paying peasants. Second, it made land unmarketable. The new regime wanted the land to be saleable, so that land price would rise, rich people would buy land, and the zamindars would turn from warlords to pure landowners. If they did not do a good job as a landlord, they would sell, and land would pass on to the most efficient producer. Both the state and the owner would gain. This was all a part of what was in the 1790s quite modern thinking. The solution was to define only ownership right and take over the tax right.

A legal deed of ownership was created. Who would this ownership deed be given to? Under the Permanent Settlement in Bengal (1793), it was given to the zamindars in exchange for tax payment that was fixed forever. The Permanent Settlement was extended in the 1800s to coastal Madras and North-Western Provinces (eastern UP). The unintended consequence of the change was that many landlords borrowed too much, became bankrupt, and sold and divided the estates. In the end, they ceased to be a military threat. But they did not prove to be efficient cultivators either. When territories in the rest of India fell into British hands in the early nineteenth century, land reforms were done on a different basis. In these regions, people like the zamindars were rare. Under the arrangement here, peasant cultivators became tax-paying owners, subject to a tax revision every 30 years. This system was known as ryotwari. In an important variation of ryotwari, in areas around Delhi, dominant kin groups were recognized as the proprietary body. The joint-landlords of village lands were collectively responsible for tax payment (Map 2.3).

The fiscal and military power of the state increased. What was this power used for? It was used to build a big central army, as mentioned. As the rule consolidated, the government paid more attention to institutions and infrastructure. There was not yet a coherent policy behind these actions. The engineering staff of the army advised the government on major infrastructure projects. If these projects were cheap to build and yet added to revenue, the government listened. Flood control by the construction of river embankments in Bengal was one such field. A bigger field was canal irrigation.

When the Company took control of the upper Gangetic plains, a network of irrigation channels was discovered there. Clearly, water management engaged all past regimes in this hot and dry land. In the older cities, there were sophisticated systems of lifting and channelling river water to the palace complex and sometimes residents. In South India, the 'grand anicut' on the Cauvery, attributed to the Chola rulers, was another large pre-British system. South India also contained huge manmade lakes or tanks. These projects were in disrepair from before Company's rule began. The Company restored some of them. The restored canals were located on the Ganges and Jamuna (1817–1840s), the deltas of the Cauvery (the 1830s and 1840s), Godavari and Krishna (1840s and 1850s).

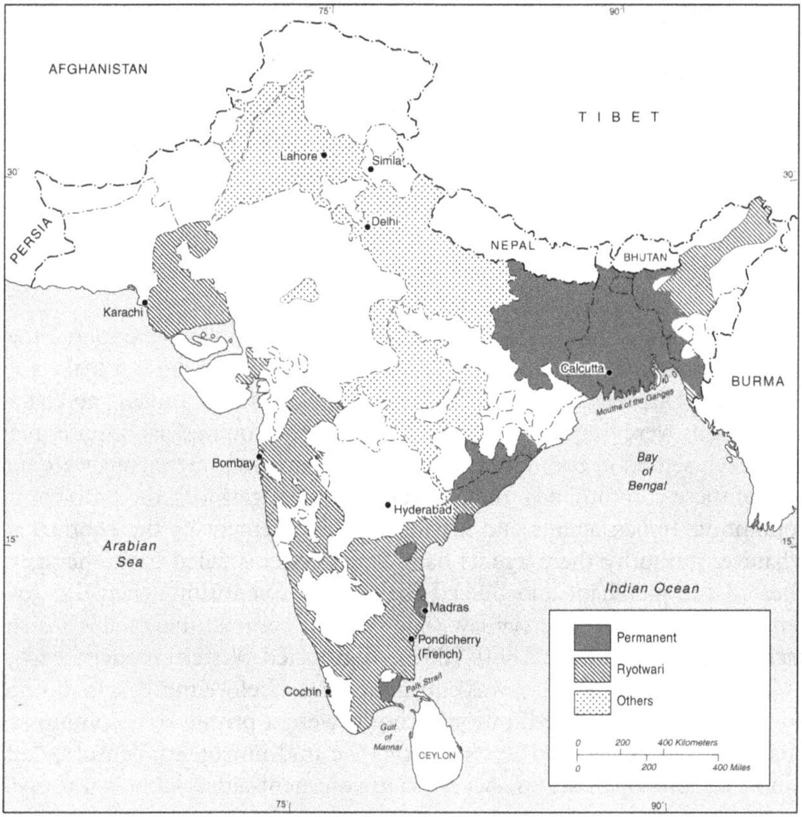

Map 2.3 Types of land settlement, 1858

Besides raising revenue, the Company wanted to sponsor trade. The first field of action was the chaotic currency system. In 1799, the Company first considered the introduction of a uniform currency for territories under its control. At that time, major currencies in circulation included the Bengal silver rupee, the Arcot silver rupee, and the Madras gold pagoda. Apart from these, many states issued their own currencies, and local exchanges happened in copper coins or seashells (cowries). In 1835, a Company silver rupee of uniform weight was introduced throughout the region. The announced exchange rate between the rupee and the pound sterling was 15:1.

The second field of reform that served both property and commerce was law. When it started its rule, the officers and intellectuals advising the government thought they had found in Sanskrit and Persian-Arabic codebooks the basis for a common law for India, as in England. The government made laws following the indigenous rulebooks. By the 1830s, the project was in trouble. The indigenous books did not represent a living jurisprudence. They were created by Brahmins for the benefit of the kings, were loaded with edicts that favoured the Brahmins, like they must be fed before others during a famine. No one knew how much of the codes the kings in fact followed.

In commercial law, indigenous codes failed completely, among other reasons because the Brahmins did not do commerce and did not make sensible laws. Disputes between European merchants and Indian merchants and artisans were frequent. Among Indians, some commercial disputes may have been settled in community courts. But immigrant merchants were not part of these communities. Indo-European trade dealt with the problem by appointing Indian agents and leaving the enforcement of the contract to whatever authority these agents had. These systems failed too. The agent cheated the merchant and bullied the artisan. Eventually, when the government created commercial law (like laws on contract, negotiable instruments, and companies in 1850–1880), it imported Western models.

The third field of action was education. India before the British did not have a system of mass education. Schools were a private or a community affair and not open to everyone. From the mid-nineteenth century, education became open access. Access to government-aided schools was open to all, though, in reality, many sorts of discrimination between men and women or upper and lower castes persisted. What the schools taught was earlier decided by the profession of the community that ran schools. The content now became standardized. To what standard was it standardized?

In 1835, Thomas Babington Macaulay (1800–1859), historian, poet, politician, and an adviser to the government on law wrote a 'minute' setting out the reasons why the government should sponsor only a westernized curriculum. The minute became infamous because Macaulay dismissed Indian learning as worthless displaying his ignorance of Indian learning. But the message had powerful backers among wealthy Indians. They believed that Macaulay's emphasis on *useful* knowledge over religion and literature was a good one, as it would give better preparation to young people for working in the modern economy. Government spending on education increased, but private sponsorship to the new system increased more. These sponsors forgave Macaulay his ignorance. They put their money in institutions that implemented the message of his minute.

As more people prepared to join a commercial economy, trade was growing. What goods were traded?

New Trades

Two big trades—textile and grain trade—declined in the late eighteenth century. But both revived quickly as British power consolidated in the fertile Indo-Gangetic Basin. In regions located near the river Ganges, there was little disturbance. Cities such as Benares, Patna, Murshidabad, or Dhaka, did well commercially. Demand for grain in growing cities like Calcutta was buoyant. In the western-Gangetic plains, some regions specialized in the production of indigo and cotton and purchased grain from areas situated further away.

By 1820, protectionism and technological change in England reduced the market for Indian cloth in Britain. The Company was not trading much anymore. But trade in the port cities was booming. The average annual growth rate of foreign trade was 4–5% during 1834–1913. The rate of growth of national income was much smaller between 1821 and 1871.[9] The composition of trade changed. Textiles (in export) and silver (in import) had dominated the eighteenth-century trade. Between 1800 and 1850, silver was not a means of paying for exports, British machine-made textiles and iron goods paid for exports. And the export basket changed from textiles to natural-resource-based goods like indigo, opium, silk, tobacco, cotton, salt, sugar, and saltpetre.

The world trade in indigo rose after the establishment of a machine textile industry in England. At first, supplies came from the West Indies. This source became uncertain during the Napoleonic wars. Since Bengal had conditions suitable for its cultivation, European capitalists invested in indigo production in the Bengal countryside. They were called 'planters', though most of them did not actually own plantations. Rather, they owned an indigo factory in a large village, advanced money to peasants, and made them sign contracts that specified the extent of land to be sown with indigo. European trading firms of Calcutta funded them, and handled marketing and shipment. The contracts left prices to be fixed by convention. In the 1850s, the price of rice increased faster than indigo, and in 1859–1860, the peasants turned unwilling to sow indigo. The chaos that followed was known as the blue mutiny. The administration refused to bail out the planters but designed a contract law instead.

Opium was an old crop in Benares, Bihar, and central India. Private traders and Company officers were aware of the huge potential market for the product in China, and the administration was keen to control the trade to capture more revenue from it (Fig. 2.2). In the late 1700s, European merchants on the southern China coast, who had seen the popularity of opium shops in the coastal towns, tried to control the trade in opium. Ships now plied between Calcutta and

Fig. 2.2 Opium warehouse in Patna (1882). Looking like library stacks, the storage space shows the immense scale of the trade from eastern India and the extent of the government's involvement in it (© Artokoloro Quint Lox Limited/ Alamy Stock Photo)

Canton. Floating depots of opium sold some of the goods locally and delivered the bulk to Chinese junks that journeyed up the rivers to sell to opium shops and overland traders. The trade was illegal, but a weak Chinese state could not stop it. The tension between the state and the foreign merchants broke out in the Opium War of 1839–1840 when large quantities of opium were seized and destroyed by the authorities. The war ended with the Treaty of Nanking (1842). Under the terms of the treaty, foreign traders would enjoy concessions and immunity from local law. The treaty also led to the transfer of Hong Kong to Britain.

Between 1780 and 1833 the Company and thereafter private traders invested on average more than a million pound sterling each year in buying tea in Canton. The tea could be purchased from the proceeds of opium after 1800. The resultant international exchange of stimulants—tea for opium—balanced trades of three countries, India, Britain, and China. Opium trade helped the Indian business. The Parsis of Bombay and Calcutta and the Marwari merchants involved in the inland trade in central Indian opium made money in it. Parsis dominated Indo-China and coastal shipping, the big names being Wadia, Readymoney, Banaji, Hormusjee Dorabjee Lascari, Dady Sett, Seth Dada Nusserwanjee, and Cama. A few Bohra firms also owned ships.

Parsi dominance in short-haul shipping did not last. In 1845, an advertisement appeared in Bombay, causing a mild stir (Figs. 2.3 and 2.4). The advertiser, Forbes, announced the first steamship to ply on a route and with a cargo that the Indian merchants of Bombay and Calcutta and owners of sail ships had so far controlled. There was no dramatic changeover. Both steam and sail continued in the trade, and the Indian merchants switched over to steam gradually. The Indo-European firm Forbes, like Fairlie-Ferguson of Calcutta, fell into a pattern of short-haul trade that the Indians dominated. Some of their largest vessels were sailing ships, acquired from reputed Parsi shipbuilders of the late eighteenth century.

Western India had excellent timber and a local shipbuilding tradition. But the knowledge, capital, and the drive to build larger ships fit to go beyond the Indian Ocean often owed to an Indo-European collaboration in the Company ports. Occasionally, Cochin, Bombay, and Moulmein attracted European artisans, like Duncan Dunbar of Moulmein, who believed that locally built ships could give the British ones a run for their

FOR CHINA.

The fine new steam-propeller barque, 'EDITH' 407 tons and 80 h.p. Geo. W. Lewis, Commdr., will sail on the 2nd August.

The vessel has excellent accommodation for passengers.

For freight, opium only, and passage, apply to FORBES AND Co.

Fig. 2.3 Advertisement in a Bombay journal, 1845 (*Source* W. H. Coates, *The Old 'Country Trade' of the East Indies*, London: Imray, Laurie, Norie, and Wilson, 1911, 84. Author's collection)

money. A few prominent Parsi families who understood timber trade and carpentry joined the business around 1780 and developed a successful apprenticeship in shipbuilding.

Opium trade fell from the 1880s, unable to stand an international campaign against opium smoking. Mainly Christian missionaries hoping to gather followers in China campaigned against opium, calling the habit immoral, a social problem, and unhealthy. This moralistic hyperbole had no relation to facts. There were plenty of opium dens in Bombay and Madras towns. Narcotics officers and doctors visited these places and made reports, and the reports found nothing alarming about them. A cross-section of society, mainly middle-income service workers spending long times out of home (such as cab drivers) went to these places to have a good time. There was no evidence of debilitating addiction among them or of serious health problems. Alcohol was a far more unhealthy addiction. The situation in China could not have been much worse.

Prudery won. But not without a fight. The missionaries made it seem that the merchants who had been doing the trade for generations were somehow a wicked type of people. This a section of Bombay's business elite and intelligentsia were not going to accept meekly. A Parsi, Rustam Cawasji, produced a scathing report attacking the 'anti-opiumists', citing

Fig. 2.4 House of Forbes. The photograph shows the offices of one of the larger European trading firms of early nineteenth-century Bombay, and a partner of the Company administration in the city (© DeGolyer Library, Southern Methodist University, William Johnson Photographs of Western India)

doctors and scientists with experience in the field. He was absolutely right to say that there was little proof of health hazards from moderate intake of opium. But he fought a losing battle.

Cotton was a third commodity to do well in trade. Descriptions of the Arabian Sea trade before European entry sometimes recorded trade in Indian cotton, though the trade was probably not large. This was to change. Cotton export to Europe began from the second half of the eighteenth century as cotton spinning expanded in Britain. Cotton was not an indigenous crop in Britain. As the production of cotton goods expanded rapidly between 1760 and 1800, annual cotton imports into Britain increased from 2000 to 280,000 tonnes. Nearly 90% of this quantity came from the United States. The Company wanted to sell

Fig. 2.5 American Civil War Interrupted England's Cotton Supply. This cartoon from the 1860s shows a confused British merchant watching the battle in the United States, while a patient Indian trader stands in front of a cotton depot waiting to be noticed (© World History Archive/Alamy Stock Photo)

Indian cotton, sponsored surveys, invited American planters to India, but did not make a success of the trade. The problems were many. The quality of ginning was poor, and inland transport cost high. The Napoleonic wars forced the British industry to use Indian cotton, and after the American civil war (1861–1866), Indian cotton was the mainstay of the British industry (Fig. 2.5). This trade was firmly in Indian hands.

As Britain industrialized, trade in manufactured goods rose. The early nineteenth century was a traumatic time for the handicrafts, because of the import of British machine-made textiles and iron. If this import hurt the artisans, for the merchants, imports were not bad news at all. The massive fall in yarn and cloth prices enabled the poor to buy more cloth.

Further, a big part of British cloth was for specific varieties. In other varieties, the hand-weaver carried on. Similarly, in iron, much of the demand was for cannons, guns, cutlery, or construction material, which the Indian artisans did not make on a large scale.

Such were the trades. Who were the traders?

Shifts in Capital

The rise of the Company regime ended the career of some of the old Indian firms, especially those who were too dependent on regional states for the services they sold. A famous example of decline was the Jagat Seth, a firm in Bengal licenced to convert currencies and perform some functions of a mint. But these were exceptional cases. Overall, Indian merchants and bankers seemed to do well, though their centre of gravity shifted towards the ports and towards commodity trade.

In the early-1800s, the trading communities prominent in the Indo-Gangetic Basin, were the Khatris, the Lohanas, and Bhatias, and among the Muslims, the Khojas and the Parachas. They did overland trade with Central Asia and Afghanistan and sometimes joined local administration. Marwaris of western Rajasthan were by contrast mainly moneylenders, who sometimes did trade. None of these groups played a significant role in maritime trade. They continued to operate in commercial centres connected by overland trade routes.

Hindu and Muslim trading communities in Gujarat and Saurashtra conducted not only inland trade, but also maritime trade between the Gujarat coast of India and the Persian Gulf, Arabia, Africa, and Malabar. The seafaring merchants of Kachchh were major players in the Arabian Sea trade, had well-developed institutions of commerce and banking, knowledge of the seas, shipping, and shipbuilding, a history of collaborating with local states, and access to both maritime and overland trade routes. In South India, the Telugu-speaking Komatis and the Tamil-speaking Chettis were the main trading communities. In eastern India, members of the Subarna Banik caste group, who had earlier traded in the Bay of Bengal and the delta, joined Indo-European trade, made money, and invested that money into education, real estate, and zamindari estates. Parsis of Bombay and Surat were traditionally not traders or financiers, but artisans, carpenters, weavers, and shipbuilders. Their entry into trade was a result of their contact with the Europeans as agents (also called broker and dubash).

The Indian agents of European companies were men who commanded wealth and influence. We know something about their influence from the accounts that two of them left behind. In the 1710s, the Parsi merchant Rustam Manock (d. 1721) of Surat was the British East India Company's broker. A part of his correspondence with the Company survives and was republished. There is also a long poem in Persian called Qisseh-i-Rustam-Manock, composed in 1710–1711 by Jamshed Kaikobad, the tutor of Nowrozji, Manock's third son. Nowrozji was the first Parsi to go to London in 1723. The second figure is Ananda Ranga Pillai (1709–1761), chief broker of the French East India Company in the 1740s, whose multi-volume diary was translated and published.

These documents do not tell us much about the individuals concerned. Manock's papers refer to disputes between his sons and the Company over money the latter owed the firm, and the unstable political situation in Surat. Pillai's diary, though supposedly a personal document, is filled with mundane details of his family and friends. But they do illustrate the huge geographical range of their operation, command over resources, and relation with other local merchants. The poem says that Manock's influence as a mediator was used by the ruler of Surat when the merchant Osman Chalebi's ship was hijacked by a Portuguese group. Manock was summoned for help since the Portuguese 'are enamoured of your name'.[10]

European traders owned the biggest firms in Calcutta in the 1800s. Some were newcomers. Others had a longer antecedent. The Company operated under a royal charter that granted it a monopoly of trade, but the monopoly was not always enforceable. Private merchants defied it and could get away because the local kings who had the policing power were not keen to use it for the benefit of one faction of Europeans against another. Besides, private traders sometimes formed clandestine business partnerships with Company employees. The London directors knew this, but beyond occasional penalties, could do little.

After the monopoly charter ended in 1813, private traders operated more freely. They were now trading in opium, indigo, silk, foreign textiles, and sugar. They were also engaged in a limited way in banking and insurance. Until about 1834, they received deposits of Company officials attracted by the high interest rates and the exchange rates on remittances. The demand and price of indigo were notoriously unstable. A violent crash in the early 1830s drove many of these to the wall. Thereafter, deposits of Company officials dried up. The European businesses began to rely more on Indian partners for capital and management.

A few of the partners set up their own firms. The Bengali Subarna Banik succeeded dramatically. The huge mansions of merchant families left intact in north Calcutta now, belonging to Mullick, Law, Ramdulal Dey (1752–1825), and Tagore, bear witness to the success. The notable firms were, Dwarakanath Tagore (1794–1846), Rustomji Cowasji, Motilal Seal (1792–1854), and the Prawnkissen Law family. Seal and Law were Subarna Baniks. The firm Carr Tagore was the largest in scale and had the most diversified interests. Using his official connections with the government, and friendships with British entrepreneurs, Dwarakanath was able to develop a major financial and commercial house. His interests included colliery, tea, salt, steamboats, indigo, and a bank. His own zamindari estate grew indigo. His bank, the Union Bank, dominated the financing of the indigo trade. Some of these partnerships ended in 1846–1847 when the Union Bank collapsed due to fraud. After this date, Bengali moneyed people tended to invest in zamindari.

Historians sometimes see this shift from trade to land as a failure of Bengali entrepreneurship, and as something rooted in the anti-business mentality of the Bengali. The shift can be explained in two other ways, one negative and one positive, and none ethnic. First, these firms traded a lot but were supported by a weak banking system. The banking business was too dependent on lending to one or two commodity trades, and money was expensive. Second, many wealthy Bengalis turned towards educating their children in the new colleges and universities that came up in Calcutta. The service industry became the new field of enterprise, in which the Bengali upper class including the progeny of the merchant families succeeded dramatically when compared with the more convention-bound merchants like the Marwaris. The Parsis of Bombay made a similar choice. Both communities lost interest in staying purely commercial but excelled as doctors, lawyers, scientists, engineers, managers, and teachers.

Merchant wealth sometimes went into industry, the Tagore firm was an example. More often, artisans set up industrial enterprises in the early 1800s. European artisans travelled to India to make a career after the end of the Company's charter in 1813. Some of them set up ironworks after the English model. A Scottish iron-master, Andrew Duncan, for example, set up a charcoal-using smelting factory in the Birbhum district of Bengal about 1810. In Bengal, South India, and Kumaon, several other ventures in iron smelting started. The most famous one was established in the river port Porto Novo by an iron-master Josiah Marshall

Heath in 1825. This enterprise produced good quality iron, and the Company thought it was worth supporting, but it never made money. None of the others did either. One problem was the high cost of wood-fuel as forests receded. Transportation from longer distances was expensive in the absence of good roads and railways.

European artisans of Bombay, Madras, and Calcutta succeeded more in making consumer goods for the European population of these cities, like horse carriages and furniture, watches, clocks, shoes, and glassware. These skills and the tastes eventually spread to the Indian artisans and consumers of these cities as well. European-style furniture, for example, changed notions of interior decoration in Indian households. Around 1800, bigger enterprises started on the Calcutta river-bank, such as ship-building yard and a cotton mill.

Just when the new state should have felt secure, it faced a serious threat.

The Mutiny and Its Aftermath

The Mutiny broke out in May 1857 in isolated military camps, and before it was suppressed in the monsoon months of 1858, had developed into a civilian resistance to Company's rule over Indian territories. The rebellion was mainly fought by professional soldiers of the Indian infantry regiments. Civilian rebellion was sporadic. Merchants and bankers rarely joined the rebellion, most tacitly helped the British. The affected regions were northern and central India, whereas the port cities remained passive, or helped the British move soldiers, goods and money.

Because of these differences, a single theory of the rise and fall of the rebellion cannot work. There was dissatisfaction in the army. Until the final Maratha wars (1818), the distance between the Indian soldiers and the European commanders in the Company army had been relatively close. In the 30 years of peace that followed, the hierarchy hardened. The doctrine of lapse fed resentment towards the British and made the revolt violent in the newly acquired Awadh and Jhansi. On the other side, many Indian merchants and bankers did not feel compelled to help the feudal lords and jeopardize their own economic ties with the port cities.[11] Merchants did not see foreign rule as foreign rule mainly, but as a useful rule. Calling this episode a 'war of independence'—as some would prefer—maybe a grand gesture but has little relation with real history.

The rebellion led to major shifts in governance and policy. The government announced a halt to further territorial acquisition. Some historians say that the government also turned more conservative in the matter of institutional intervention. This is not true. In fact, it passed a huge number of new laws protecting commercial and peasant property, including major tenancy and debt laws. A correct assessment would be that there was now greater caution about empowerment of landlords in the countryside, whereas the state became more concerned to protect tenant rights against landlords, and encourage trade and industry.[12]

In 1858, the Crown took over the administration of British India.

Conclusion

Historians debate whether the time between the two empires was a time of decline or growth. In one view there was a decline because the fall of the Mughal Empire weakened state power and reduced the wealth of merchants who depended on the state. In another view, it was a time of growth because the successor states gave merchants new business and more power. The contrast between these two scenarios is overdrawn because economic and business growth needs *both* strong states and free enterprise. Successor states may have given merchants more room to grow, but they were not strong and stable enough to promote business. On the other hand, there is no evidence at all that the countryside was either worse off or better off during the passage of empires.

In one field and only one field, there was a dramatic change. One set of cities declined and another rose in wealth.

Compared with cities in the interior like Agra, Delhi, Poona (Pune), Murshidabad or Lucknow, the Company ports presented merchants with a distinctly better alternative. They were well-protected places and became magnets for migrant Indian merchants. At 1850, the only large hubs of business where trade was free and state protection strong enough were Bombay, Madras, and Calcutta, recently joined by Karachi, and towns that had deep links with these places, like Ahmedabad, Kanpur, and Baroda. The main activity of these cities was the trade in agricultural commodities that came from inland.

How did trading cities like these change in the years after the Mutiny?

Notes

1. J.F. Richards, *The Mughal Empire*, Cambridge: Cambridge University Press, 1995.
2. Irfan Habib, 'The Eighteenth Century in Indian Economic History', in P.J. Marshall, ed., *The Eighteenth Century in Indian History,* New Delhi: Oxford University Press, 2003, 100–119; M. Athar Ali, 'Recent Theories of Eighteenth Century India,' in Marshall, ed., *The Eighteenth Century*, 90–99.
3. Burton Stein, 'A Decade of Historical Efflorescence,' *South Asia Research*, 10, 1990, 125–138.
4. Stephen Broadberry, Johann Custodis and Bishnupriya Gupta, 'India and the Great Divergence: An Anglo-Indian Comparison of GDP Per Capita, 1600–1871,' *Explorations in Economic History*, 55(1), 2015, 58–75.
5. Doab, the tract between two confluent rivers.
6. Holden Furber, Review of A. Mervyn Davies, *Clive of Plassey: A Biography*, New York: Charles Scribner's Sons, 1939, *American Historical Review*, 45(3), 1940, 635–637.
7. Tirthankar Roy, *East India Company: The World's Most Powerful Corporation*, New Delhi: Allen Lane, 2012.
8. M. Oak and A.V. Swamy, 'Myopia or Strategic Behavior? Indian Regimes and the East India Company in Late Eighteenth Century India,' *Explorations in Economic History* 49(3), 2012, 352–366.
9. GDP at current prices increased by about 25% between 1821 and 1871, based on Broadberry, Custodis and Gupta, 'India and the Great Divergence: An Anglo-Indian Comparison of GDP Per Capita, 1600–1871.
10. Jivanji Jamshedji Modi, 'Rustam Manock (1635–1721 A.C.) the Broker of the English East India Company, and the Persian Qisseh (History) of Rustam Manock. A Study,' *Asiatic Papers*, Bombay: Times of India Press, 1929, 101–280.
11. Tirthankar Roy, 'The Mutiny and the Merchant,' *The Historical Journal*, 59(2), 2016, 393–416.
12. Tirthankar Roy and Anand V. Swamy, *Law and the Economy in Colonial India*, Chicago: Chicago University Press, 2016.

Further Reading

Burton Stein, ed., 'Introduction', *The Making of Agrarian Policy in British India 1770–1900*, Delhi: Oxford University Press, 1992, 1–32.

Kenneth McPherson, *The Indian Ocean: A History of People and the Sea*, New York: Oxford University Press, 1998.

Om Prakash, *European Commercial Enterprise in Precolonial India: The New Cambridge History of India*, Cambridge: Cambridge University Press, 1998.

P.J. Marshall (ed.), 'Introduction', *Eighteenth Century in Indian History: Evolution or Revolution?* Delhi: Oxford University Press, 2003, 1–30.

Tirthankar Roy, *An Economic History of Early Modern India*, London and Abingdon: Routledge, 2013.

CHAPTER 3

The Business of the Cities

Abstract Colonial India was a trading economy. Financial and industrial development happened to serve the needs of commodity trade and with profits from commodity trade. Capitalists prominent in this business system usually had a stake in all three and spread risks between the three. They did not stop with earning money. Leading business families spent their money on public goods and took part in politics. The port cities and their satellites were not only hubs of enterprise, but also hubs of education. They were sites where self-government was first put into practice. What was this business world like?

Keywords Business history of India · Industrialization · Capitalism · Business community · Philanthropy in India

Colonial India was a trading economy. The major part of the trade consisted of trade in agricultural commodities, which needed the railways and made the railways profitable. Factories were an extension of commodity trade, being built with the profits of trade. Since banking was also tied to trade, the business system that emerged between 1860 and 1940 was based on an integration of trade, banking, and industry. Capitalists prominent in this business system usually had a stake in all three and spread risks between the three.

© The Author(s) 2019

T. Roy, *How British Rule Changed India's Economy*,
Palgrave Studies in Economic History,
https://doi.org/10.1007/978-3-030-17708-9_3

They did not stop with earning money. Leading business families also spent their money on public goods and took part in politics. The port cities and their satellites were not only hubs of enterprise, but also hubs of education. They were sites where self-government was first put into practice.

This chapter discusses this business world and shows why it could deliver productivity growth (Fig. 1.1).

Trade

The volume of long-distance trade in India grew more than a hundred-fold between 1860 and 1940 (Fig. 3.1). The government helped that process by maintaining open borders to goods, labour, and capital. Cities like Bombay, Ahmedabad, Madras, Calcutta, Kanpur, and Karachi, when linked to the agricultural interior by railways and telegraph, received and exported cotton, indigo and opium at first, and later exported or

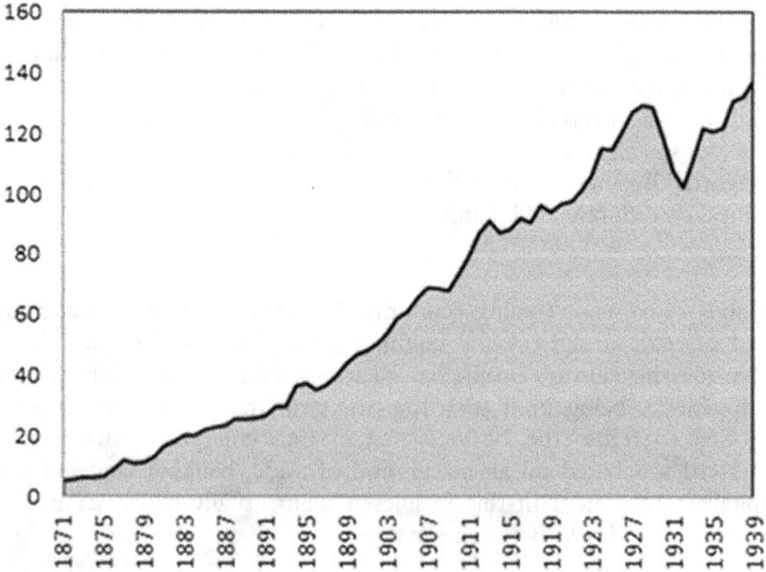

Fig. 3.1 Trade volume (million tons cargo through railways and ports) (Source: *Statistical Abstracts for British India*, various years)

redistributed foodgrain, textiles, machinery, metals, and chemicals. These cities hired foreigners to work in the factories, banks, and trading firms. Merchant families migrated to these cities. Merchant houses based here had branches in the rest of India, and sometimes in Southeast and East Asia, Africa, and Europe.

Europeans conducted a part of this trade. They were especially prominent in that part of commodity trade going abroad. British firms or those like Sassoon or Ralli with strong links to Britain were the main players. Their British partners and subsidiaries took care of sale abroad, supplied capital, and sent managers to work in India. Some firms set up by people like Charles Forbes, Thomas Parry (1768–1824) and James Finlay (1727–1792) emerged around 1800. Others arrived in the 1850s and the 1860s. The partners of Greaves Cotton started as a trader in cotton and textile machinery around 1850. The family of David Sassoon (1792–1864) was Turkish Jews who shifted base to Bombay around 1840. Sassoon inherited his father's trading firm, which carried on business in Persian, Indian, and British goods, and later moved to China to trade Indian goods there. In Cochin in Kerala, Robert H. Peirce and Patrick Leslie formed Peirce, Leslie, and Co. in 1862 to trade in Malabar spices. A few years later, John Aspinwall set up a trading and shipping firm in Cochin. In the 1840s, the Wallace family entered the India trade in Burma teak. In 1851, Salomon Volkart (1816–1893), a commodity trader moved from the Mediterranean to Bombay, and the Greek merchant Pantia Ralli (1793–1865) set up an operation in Calcutta. Volkart dominated Indian cotton export and Ralli wheat export.

A late addition to this set of foreign trading companies was the Japanese merchant. The first Japanese trading firms arrived in the 1890s. They took advantage of the competitive shipping industry, efficient information exchange between Bombay and Osaka, the partnership with Indian businesses (Tata in Bombay and Andrew Yule in Calcutta were among the partners), and the presence of Indian merchants in Kobe, Singapore, and Hong Kong. In the interwar period partnership between the Japanese Sogo Sosha and Indian merchants developed even more. The former set was keen to buy Indian cotton and had success in selling textiles in India.

Other Indo-European trading firms included a small set of produce brokers (J. Thomas, Carritt-Moran), who performed a crucial service in the sale of tea, certify quality; those dealing in artisanal goods like carpets and Madras Handkerchiefs (Brunschweiler, Gordon Woodroffe,

Arbuthnot of Madras, Tellery in Mirzapur); and importers of chemicals, metals, and machines. Platt Brothers were the largest suppliers of cotton mill machinery until the advent of ring spindles. Leading British firms set up importing offices in India around 1920. By 1920, there were a string of British engineering companies, which exported to India, at the same time looking to expand manufacturing in India, for example, Calcutta's Metal Box and Guest Keen Williams.

In the twentieth century, the range of consumer goods imported from Britain expanded to include new articles like cosmetics, sewing machines, processed food, bicycles, and cars. Trading agencies of foreign manufacturers tried to create a consumer base. The Indian subsidiary of the food processing firm Unilever was an example. The household chemicals firm Reckitt and Colman started a trading unit in India in the 1920s. Imperial Tobacco Company in India started as a subsidiary of British American Tobacco in 1910. Selling these goods to the Indians was a challenging task, performed with the help of Indian agents. Agency of this kind was a field of innovative entrepreneurship.

Among Indian businesses, grain and cotton trades made the fortunes of many Gujarati merchants and bankers in Bombay. A lot of good cotton was grown in the South Gujarat coast. The trade interlinked Bombay, Broach (Bharuch), and Ahmedabad. In towns along the coast, merchants invested in gins and spinning mills. Grain trade was spread out even more and penetrated most villages in India. A hierarchy of agents lived in the railway towns, went into the village markets to buy grain or cotton on behalf of bigger merchants.

Money flowed into local trades during the busy season in the form of bankers' drafts or hundis drawn in the big city. Railway invoice could be cashed too. The merchants and their agents owned carts, grain pits, and warehouses, and sometimes successfully persuaded the corporate bank of the city to open cash credit accounts for them on the security of the crop. There were few Europeans in this world, though in the larger markets some firms had European partners and owners. Agents and employees of big foreign houses like Volkart, Ralli, or Toyo Menka could neither displace nor operate without the help of Indian agents, so entrenched was their position. And they were so strong in local trade because they knew peasants and landlords personally.

Much of the grain and cotton for trade passed through Bombay, Karachi, Calcutta, and Madras. This was so because these cities had already developed as railway hubs. The railways were crucial to the grain trade not only because they reduced costs of trade, but they also carried price information. An inland merchant had limited access to price information, except by coming to a railway town where large-scale business took place near the railway station.

What about finance?

Finance

Financial development in colonial India is a story of success and failure. Its success was in funding the enormous increase in commodity trade. Its failure was in the limited help that banks gave to fixed investment in industry. The success cannot be understood without failure. Money was rationed in industrial finance because it was put more profitably to trading. Some historians (like Morris D. Morris) suggest that trade offered a higher rate of return, and Indians put more money there for that reason. This is not wholly true. Trade involved a distinct set of risks. A lot of the credit transactions in commodity trade occurred without legal contracts and collaterals. The clients were people of small means, who would not be able to repay if a crop failed or there was a marriage in the family. These transactions demanded high returns because they carried high default risk. Only people with personal knowledge of clients could operate in this field. Corporate banks and Europeans were not good for that job.

If banks took lesser risks, their business ought to grow faster. Corporate banking did grow rapidly. The proportion of corporate bank deposit in national income increased from zero to 12% in 1860–1940. But banks had limitations too. They would not lend to people without security and paperwork, and officers knew few of their clients personally. Corporate banks financed a few big traders and bankers who lent money to local commodity trade. Banks recognized the bills and hundies that some of these houses issued. Rarely did they go further than that.

Despite the increased supply of credit, interest rates were high. The tropical monsoon climate created a short cultivation season and a long slack season. The conduct of agriculture in these conditions was marked by extreme seasonal fluctuations in demand for money. At the start of harvest and sowing seasons, loans needed to be advanced to a vast army of local merchants suddenly, for short periods, among clients who were too far away from banks, and who could not read documents. Cheques and drafts would not work in this system, only cash would. Because of the huge and sudden spike in demand, interest rates rose to astronomical levels during the busy season (November–March), and since money was hoarded during the slack season in readiness for the busy season, little was available for industry.

Among corporate banks, there was one set that need not concern us much. These were the so-called Presidency banks, the Bank of Bengal, Bank of Bombay and Bank of Madras. Established between 1809 and 1843, these had participation by the government in the capital, and government control on management. These banks held the government's cash balances, issued (on a limited scale) and circulated currency notes, discounted bills and securities, advanced short-term working capital credit to private business, and accepted deposits from the public. They did play a role in the private money market. But the government ties made both their operations and management different from other corporate banks. Their share in the business fell too.

Practically all other corporate banks, including the exchange banks licensed to deal in foreign exchange, mainly funded commodity trade, especially movements of goods between cities, big railway stations, and between ports and overseas markets. The most successful among these dealt with established large firms. Others were less fussy and lent money to or discounted bills issued by moneylenders, landlords, wealthy urban residents, and sometimes small-scale industry.

Indians understood overland trade better than the Europeans did. Therefore, Indian-owned banks dominated the corporate banking scene. Whenever trading conditions improved, a banking boom began. Thus, cotton speculation in Bombay in the 1860s encouraged banking. Most of the banks then started later went into liquidation. The spread of the spirit of swadeshi or self-reliance from 1906 encouraged a mini-banking boom around Calcutta. In 1913–1914, a few major bankruptcies led to a widespread crash of these banks. The end of World War I encouraged another banking boom, which ended in a crash in 1923. The business was so unstable because the attraction of investing in high-risk and high-return fields was great. Many smaller banks did not have enough reserves and were exposed to one or two local trades. Banks run by families that also traded were prone to insider lending. And there was no regulator nor a lender-of-last-resort yet.

The instability of the business marked a few banks out from the rest, those that could weather the risks thanks to prudent management, deep pockets, and a conservative attitude. They held a large proportion of assets in the form of government securities, and in this respect were much like the Presidency banks. At the top of the list were Allahabad Bank, Bank of Baroda, Bank of India, Punjab National Bank, and Central Bank of India. These were established in the larger towns and emerged from existing business partnerships between large trading and industrial houses. All members of the set survive today as nationalized banks. A group of Europeans started Allahabad Bank in 1864. The Maharaja of Baroda, with the leading banking (shroff) houses of the city, started Bank of Baroda in 1908. The family of David Sassoon started Bank of India in 1906, with contributions to share capital from Parsi, Gujarati, and Bohra houses of Bombay. The Central Bank was established in 1911 by a Parsi house and merged with the Tata banking business in the 1920s. A group of traditional business houses based in Lahore started Punjab National Bank (1895). To this list should be added the Canara Bank, started by lawyers of the Goud Saraswat community, who had a tradition of community banking.

Beyond corporate banks, moneylenders ruled local finance. Many indigenous bankers issued hundi, which functioned as trade bills or a banker's draft depending on the usage. These hundis were not widely accepted outside the community networks. Besides hundis, inter-shroff short-term loans financed post-harvest crop movement. Traders borrowed from lenders who in turn borrowed from other lenders, the chain reached some of the large shroff houses whose bills were acceptable to the corporate banks. Large inter-shroff transactions were monitored by means of community channels. Personal reputation mattered to the success of the hundi. Not everybody could enter the business as clients or as banking firms. Moneylending groups like Marwaris and Chettiars had a better chance.

Most clients of the bankers and moneylenders were people in need of quick money and who could not give security. The strength of the moneylender network was its intimate knowledge of clients, which made the paperwork simpler. But then, in a remote village, a moneylender could impose an effective monopoly of finance and exploit peasants and merchants. This monopolistic aspect of market-power has drawn a lot of attention from leftist historians, who see it as a sign of exploitation. In fact, the moneylenders' exploitative power is exaggerated. The moneylender took considerable risks in lending to impoverished clients engaged in unstable livelihoods.

Chapter 2 showed that the port cities were experimenting with factories from the end of the eighteenth century. Industrialization took on a steadier aspect after Crown rule began.

Factories

Around 1860, the industrialization drive centred on the textile industry. The capital came from trading profits and foreign investment. Bombay and Calcutta benefited from the growth of India's trade with China after the Company's monopoly in China trade ended (1833). Profits of cotton and opium trades were invested in a cotton mill industry in Western India. In Calcutta, foreign investment came in a steadier flow after Crown takeover.

Between 1865 and 1914, the number of cotton spinning and weaving factories in Bombay Island and Ahmedabad rose from 20 to 271, and average daily employment to 260,000. By 1914, 40% of the employment was spread in smaller towns, often far away from these hubs. Any small town that had a cotton market, a railway connection, a pool of migrant labour, and a handloom industry, became an attractive site for a spinning mill. Using these strengths Kanpur, Madurai, Coimbatore, Sholapur, Nagpur and a string of cotton trading towns in the Deccan developed cotton mills.

In these years, cotton mills were mainly selling yarn to handloom weavers in India and China. In both these markets, Indian yarn put an end to the hand-spinning of cotton, and successfully competed with British yarn in the coarser varieties. But the Indian mills found it difficult to compete in the finer varieties and later, with Japan. In the 1890s, newly established Japanese mills took over the China market. The loss of the China market and keener Japanese competition in India forced the mills of Bombay, in the interwar period, to weave more of their own yarn into cloth, spin and weave finer yarn, improve efficiency at the workplace and save on labour. For some mills that were poorly managed, these changes came too late. The interwar period saw unemployment and strikes and made the millowners nationalistic, anti-Japan, and protectionist. The rulers of India shared the anti-Japan sentiment and granted tariffs.

Jute is a natural fibre grown mainly in southern West Bengal and Bangladesh. It is used as a raw material for sacking cloth. The demand for sacks increased in the nineteenth century with growth in international commodity trade. Until the 1870s, Bengal raw jute was processed into sacking mainly in Dundee in Britain, and somewhat later in Germany. But already mechanized jute spinning and weaving had started near Calcutta. Scottish capitalists relocated their business from Scotland to Calcutta. Between 1869 and 1913, the number of mills increased from 5 to 64, and employment from 5–10,000 to 215,000. Until World War I, the industry was owned and managed by Europeans.

Tea was another industry in which European investment came in on a large scale. When the Company lost its monopoly of China trade (1833), it turned to India for supplies of tea. Assam, which had become part of British India in 1826, had the ideal climate and topography for tea plantations. Efforts to develop plantations in Assam began. The initial experience was not good, because Assam still lacked labour and easy transport access. The labour situation improved as tea plantation companies made deals with labour contractors. The government came in with a law that made a breach of labour contract (indenture) a crime. Railway access improved too. With these developments, the area under tea gardens expanded from 154,000 acres in 1880 to 337,000 acres in 1900. The number of workers increased from 184,000 to 665,000. Gardens later came up in the Darjeeling hills and the Dooars region in north Bengal, and in the Surma valley in Eastern Bengal. Nearly 75% of tea land, however, was in Assam (Fig. 3.2). Between 1860 and 1900, tea plantations started in south India. Some tea was already grown in the Nilgiri hills. By 1900, cultivation started in the Wynaad and the Kannan-Devan hills in North Travancore.

Calcutta-based British managing agents controlled the majority of the estates and the largest of them. The main groups were Andrew Yule, McLeod, Begg-Dunlop (merged with McLeod in the interwar period), Jardine-Skinner, Octavius Steel, Williamson-Magor, Shaw Wallace, Gillanders-Arbuthnot, Davenport, and Duncan Brothers. James Finlay controlled almost the entire crop of the Kannan-Devan hills.

Tea sales were made in auctions at Calcutta and London. The participants in these auctions were 'brokers' who sampled, inspected, tasted and valued tea from the plantations. They brought tea to the auctions and gave advances to the tea growers. There were a few broker firms in Calcutta, such as J. Thomas and Carritt-Moran. All were British concerns until independence. Thanks to a three-way partnership between London auction houses, Calcutta brokers, and Assam plantation companies,

Fig. 3.2 Transporting tea. Assam was remote and badly connected when tea plantations started there. This undated photograph shows the dependence of the trade on slow modes of transport of a delicate merchandise like tea. Railway connection running through present-day Bangladesh made for a revolutionary change (© PR Archive/Alamy Stock Photo)

British capitalists dominated the business. Bengali capitalists entered the industry in the 1880s, but never dominated it. The majority of them owned small gardens in the Dooars. Most Indian firms were family firms rather than public companies.

World War I diverted the resources of the western nations into producing war supplies. The demand for cotton and jute textiles increased, but machines, metals, chemicals imported by Indian industry from Britain and Germany stopped. By the third or fourth year of the war, conditions were easier and exporting factories were making big profits. These profits gave a boost to a few new industries.

Steel was the most important example. Metallurgy had potentials in India because many raw materials for metallurgy were available, though not all the reserves were ready for commercial exploitation.

Steel was already being produced in a few mid-sized factories. The most ambitious steel producer, Tata Steel, began production from 1911. The firm of the Tatas was established in textiles and had a considerable brand name in Bombay. The Tatas were also the largest steel importer into India and knew the trade well enough to be confident of being able to produce steel at a lower cost. Still, manufacturing steel on a large scale was not easy because that required access to coal, iron, manganese, limestone, water, and transport, and would need to gather a large number of labourers, raise capital, and train workers in steel-making. The firm managed some of these difficulties, for example, it relied heavily on American engineers to run the operations. But this was not a cheap option, and the firm ran into serious problems after the War ended. In the end, the firm needed government support in getting a railway contract and tariff protection. Tata Steel carried out its first major expansion between 1925 and 1935 sheltered in this way and came out of the crisis.

Until 1918, industrialization had occurred without tariffs. Lancashire textile interests put pressure upon the Indian government to keep import duty low. The government did impose a nominal duty but neutralized it with excise duty on Indian cloth in the 1890s. It did not face much criticism, only a few cotton mill owners protested. Cotton mills did not dominate modern business, trading firms did. Because business was so diverse and all of them had a stake in trade, protection was not the preferred option for all.

The war changed the politics of protection. Until then, purchase of industrial goods for defence, railways or administrative use was dependent on Britain. This dependence had created sudden shortages of these goods during the war. Many administrators now started supporting policies to develop India industrially, seeing how Indian resources had helped the war effort. The decline in the influence of British industrial lobbies on colonial policy weakened the resistance to protection within the empire. Between 1923 and 1939, 51 enquiries were made about the suitability of demand for protective tariffs. In 11 of these cases, tariffs were raised. These included salt, heavy chemicals, magnesium chloride, sericulture, plywood chests, gold thread, iron and steel, cotton textiles, sugar, paper, and paper pulp, and matches. Thereafter, more factories in sugar, iron, and steel, cement, matches, paper, and woollen textiles were established, and the existing ones expanded.

The practical rule for granting protection was that an application for protection needed to show that the applicant would be competitive in near future. The Indian Tariff Board, the body that heard the applications, was worried about the low labour productivity in Indian manufacturing. That Indian labour managed fewer machines than their counterparts elsewhere was a well-known fact, often attributed to the poor effort at training and skill building. Skilled labour was scarce and frequently had to be hired in Britain, Germany or the United States. The mandate before the Board was to permit tariffs subject to the condition that the beneficiary would deliver efficiency improvements soon. That condition did not go down well politically. By 1940, nationalist politicians, industrialists, and economists loudly campaigned for the removal of conditions. The wind was blowing their way. Thereafter, protectionism became an entitlement for the ethnically *Indian* capital and an instrument to serve the 'national interest'. The Tariff Board was as good as dead.[1]

Depression conditions gave this campaign legitimacy. In steel, paper, sugar, and cement, Indian industry faced cheap imports and falling world prices. In the 1920s and the 1930s, the Japanese mills were selling a lot of cotton textiles in India. In steel, worldwide capacity building progressed faster than new demand, which placed the new firm, Tata Steel, in trouble. In jute, Indian capacity grew faster than world demand. The Indian nationalists argued that the rupee was overvalued to help the government balance budget (the government made foreign remittances), but the overvaluation damaged exports.

During World War II, again supplies failed and prices rose. But Indian industry in 1939 was more diversified and better equipped to diversify than in 1914. If it was not so bad for the capitalists, the war was a disaster for the workers. Prices rose. Feeding their workers became a challenging task for the plantations and industry.

Industry had to overcome the shortage of skilled labour, capital, managers, and technology. How did it overcome these shortages?

'Inputs' into Factories: Labour, Capital, Management, and Technology

An industrial firm was fundamentally different from a trading firm, which most Indian capitalists were familiar with. It needed to gather a large number of workers together and make them learn the rhythm of factory work, to raise capital that would be locked in for a long time, to hire managers when managers were scarce, and to put machinery that the workers had not seen before to work. Wages in India were low compared with the industrialized countries, and some natural resources were cheaper. But that was the only advantage. None of the other problems was easy to solve. How were they solved then?

An open labour market helped. Skilled workers in cotton, jute, steel, and other large-scale industries had a significant share of foreigners, followed by Parsis, and Hindu upper castes with high school education. 'Skilled' in this context would mean workers with some formal training or education. Between the first origins of cotton mills in Bombay, and 1925, the percentage of Europeans among the supervisory staff decreased from 100% to less than 30. Indian middle classes took to supervisory work in factories as readily as they accepted modern education.

The seasonal nature of agricultural work helped too. All other workers, who were trained on the job, came mainly from peasant families in regions where off-season job opportunities were limited. Such source regions included the Konkan, the Deccan, and United Provinces (UP) in the cotton mills, and north Bihar, eastern UP and Orissa in jute. The workers who came to the factories were not necessarily the poorest or the most distressed people of the countryside. Few among them were agricultural labourers. Most were landowning peasants. They were not among the poorest. But like the poor, they had time in their hands. Agriculture was a seasonal affair. In the slack seasons, people looked for work. Some in the textile factories had been skilled artisans before. The mills valued their skill in managing tasks that required some dexterity.

Not everybody in the same situation could come to the city. Many did because a labour contractor came to them and told them where work was available. Big men variously called sardars, jobbers, and kanganies, recruited workers, brought them to the factory and plantation sites, taught them basic skills, looked after them, lent them money, enjoyed the authority of hiring and firing people under them, and exploited them. In the plantations, once they signed a contract, the workers were trapped into fulfilling that contract thanks to the Workmen's Breach of Contract Act (1859), which made a breach of contract a criminal offence for the workers.

But as migration from the countryside to the cities became a regular flow, workers gained more control over their conditions and decisions. By the 1920s, average mill wages were considerably higher than wages everywhere else. The disparity was significant with Bombay and Calcutta.

These towns attracted many single male migrants who stood at the mill gates every morning seeking casual work when such work was becoming harder to come by.

The contractor was common in almost all societies where factories first appeared. But whereas in England, USA, or Japan, the employers took over control of personnel management, in India, the contractor continued to exist and even commanded power. That authority did not always serve the factory owners and managers well.

The economists Susan Wolcott and Gregory Clark have shown that for comparable work, Indian cotton mills employed more people than did factories in Britain, USA, Japan or China. The inefficiency did not trouble the mill owners too much while their main rivals were factories in Europe or America that paid much higher wages. When Japan, which paid smaller wages, entered the field, Indian mills found it difficult to deal with the competition. Wolcott and Clarke do not quite explain why the Indian mills employed relatively more people for similar tasks, hinting at a cultural explanation. Others have tried to explain this feature as the rational response to an economic condition.

One explanation should be obvious from old photos of factory workers. There are many group photos that date to the 1920s and the 1930s. Several of these show groups of men so different in their appearance, dress, and the tools they hold in hand that it would seem as if the photographer wanted to emphasize the ethnic diversity of the group. Inside a factory that employed several thousand people, many languages were spoken, many castes and religions were present. These differences were often preserved by the fact that one task or department hired mainly one ethnic set. Such ethnic diversity was unique to Indian factories, it did not exist in England or New England or Japan or China, only in India. Managing diversity was not a problem for factories in the West or in Japan, it was a big challenge in India. Because of this diversity, large factories continued to rely on contractors or middle-tier workers. The middle-tier were something like social leaders, recruiters, personnel managers, communicators and trainers combined. The sardars' and jobbers' authority could make it difficult for the manager to shed labour and install machines. For, it was in the middle-tier's interest to keep a larger workforce. When the crunch came, in the 1930s, workers resisted modernization, the middle-tier gave leadership to such conflicts, and only a few mills could rationalize work.

If creating a labour force was one challenge, investment was another. Interest rates were high in India. Banks and moneylenders did not lend for the long term. Although stock markets had begun in 1875, the amount invested in shares by 1940 was too little. Ordinary people did not always trust the share market because there were too much insider trade and speculation. For an Indian entrepreneur, the initial money came from the savings of a trading firm, a banking firm, or from personal borrowing within a small set of people known to each other. Invariably, therefore, the Indian pioneers came from communities that had specialized in trading and banking activities.

Parsi merchants and shipwrights of western India started the first factories, followed by merchant communities like the Khojas, Bhatias, Gujarati traders, Gujarati bankers, and Baghdadi Jews. The Parsis, who did well in Indo-China opium trade, had always been a coastal community. While the China trade declined from the late nineteenth century, prominent Parsi businesses moved to manufacture, import trade, real estate and to professions. They also held shares of big companies of the time, like the Great Indian Peninsular Railway. The owners of the first cotton mills came from these communities, with a few from European trading houses dealing in cotton. The pioneering names among cotton millowners were Petit, Wadia, and Tata (Parsis), Currimbhoys (Khojas), Sassoons (Jews), Khatau, Gokuldas, Thakersey (Bhatias from Kutchch), and Greaves Cotton, W. H. Brady and Killick Nixon (European houses). The origin of Ahmedabad's mill industry was more rooted in Hindu and Jain business. Among the prominent names, Sarabhais and Lalbhais were Jain traders and bankers.

Some European industrialists had started in India trade. For example, the Scottish firm James Finlay began in 1765 as a textile trader in Scotland, started buying cotton from India in the 1830s, started jute mills in Calcutta in the 1870s, then began selling Indian tea, and by 1900, were the biggest tea plantation company of South India. Others moved into industry directly, as many jute mill owners in Calcutta did, by selling shares in London. Others still were started by officers and artisans. A few shifted their industrial base from Scotland to Calcutta.

The combined set included Andrew Yule (jute, tea, coal, paper, engineering), Bird and F. W. Heilgers (jute, coal, engineering, limestone), McLeod-Begg-Dunlop (jute, tea, railways), Jardine-Skinner and George Henderson (jute, tea, engineering), Octavius Steel (tea, electricity), Shaw

Wallace (tea, coal), Gillanders-Arbuthnot (jute, tea, coal), Macneill-Barry (jute, coal, electricity), Martin-Burn (coal, wagons, dockyards, cement), Balmer-Lawrie (coal, paper, engineering), and Kilburn (tea, coal, engineering). Smaller groups included Kettlewell-Bullen, Mackinnon-Mackenzie, Thomas Duff (all three in jute). Two other large houses, Williamson-Magor, and Duncan Brothers, mainly owned tea estates.

Industry in Calcutta was mainly European-owned. But Indian traders based in Calcutta, chiefly the Marwaris, supplied European firms raw materials. Since the late eighteenth century, the Marwaris had steadily dispersed from their original home in Rajasthan and resettled in new business towns as moneylenders and revenue farmers. Then they began to enter trade. The history of prominent Marwari houses such as Birla, Goenka, or Jalan shows that their main interests about 1900 were in jute baling, mining, zamindari, and import agency. By 1940, these firms had entered the jute industry, and on a smaller scale entered sugar, paper, cement, construction, and share-broking.

Unlike Bombay or Calcutta, Madras offered narrower scope for factory-based industrialization. A few European companies had started as traders and ended up owning cotton and sugar mills. Among Indians, the banking community Chettiars, who went to Lower Burma to finance the rice export trade there, returned in the 1930s to invest in manufacturing. In the interwar period, the Tamil Nadu region also saw growth of small-scale industry like sugar, oil, nuts, coir, and grain mills. The main source of capital was the savings of the farmers and traders.

Like skilled labour and capital, trained managers were rare too. Most Indian companies managed their businesses by recruiting their sons and relatives into top positions. Sometimes the recruitment pool included members of the same caste or community. Most Parsi businesses in the nineteenth century recruited partners and managers from among other Parsis. A Parsi mill owner, even if he did not know a new Parsi recruit, at least knew how to find more information about the person if needed. Unorthodox partnerships cutting across caste and community did happen. But these were rare.

Reliance on the community weakened over time. In the 1870s, legislation on contracts and negotiable instruments made a formal contract between two people as secure as an informal contract based on blood or marriage ties. Inside most communities (like the Parsis), disputes between older and younger members were getting out of control.

Reputation for trade sometimes attached to whole groups. But the reputation for industry fixed upon successful companies rather than groups. Industrialization empowered individuals more than communities. The successful people set up clubs and chambers of commerce. Clubs and chambers became more important than blood or marriage ties. In these ways, the community came under increasing pressure.

Informal ties did not disappear overnight. One reason for its persistence was that laws on succession and inheritance of property recognized the undivided family. In British Indian property law, the right of a family consisting of the blood descendants of a male ancestor superseded the rights of the individuals within it. This form of property right, which the lawmakers had borrowed from Hindu code books helped business families because it enabled capital to stay undivided. At the same time, the law increased disputes within the family between younger and older members as the demand to divide property became intense just because it could be legally obstructed. The twentieth century saw an outburst of such demands among all business families.

Most European firms were managed differently. They formed partnerships among people of compatible skills or capital. As the scale of their operations expanded in the late nineteenth century, the managerial expertise would be shared via a system called managing agency. A managing agent was usually a partnership firm set up to manage other companies. The directors of the company asked the partnership firm to supply management for a fee (and sometimes commission on sales) for a fixed term. The managing agency allowed companies to raise capital from the market, without exposing themselves to takeover risk, because management control was with another firm and protected by a contract. One agency firm would manage several businesses when managers were in short supply and companies wanted to conserve and share expertise.

Indians too used managing agency, but for a different reason. Their companies were closely held and most families did not head a diversified group. Neither keeping control nor sharing managerial expertise was a big motivation. In this case, a significant role for the managing agent was raising loans and deposits. Indian firms found it hard to meet their fixed and working capital requirements out of paid-up share capital and had to rely on loans and public deposits. Loans required a guarantor, and deposits required the borrower to be a trusted and reputed name. The managing agents served these functions.

No matter who owned the agency, a corporate governance problem appeared often. If the agent's income was secure thanks to a contractual fee, why would the agent serve the interests of the shareholders? Among the Europeans, the desire to protect their reputation kept this problem under control. Several of these agents managed a dozen or more companies each, and their conduct was visible to the public. Among Indians, the problem was more serious. Families took decisions that were never recorded and never revealed to the public. Their control both over the agency and the managed company could mean that the majority shareholders could cheat the minority shareholders without risk. For example, the agents speculated in commodity trade in goods and raw materials in which the company was interested. Such speculation was often against the company's interests.

Thus, the worlds of Indian business and foreign business were quite distinct. European firms were more global, dominant in overseas trade and oceanic shipping, had easier access to joint-stock banks and the formal capital market. The Indians were dominant in overland commodity trade, produced and traded in handicrafts, used boats and carts for transportation, relied on family, caste and community ties, dominated the markets in shares and in bullion, and used indigenous bankers for remittance and capital.

The relative position of the two groups changed in the interwar period. World War I made many Indians rich. The Great Depression hit the exporting foreign firms harder than it did the Indians. Indian industrialists were gaining political power as Indian representation in politics increased. The rise of nationalism now brought these two groups into conflict. A small set of industrialists or aspiring industrialists, like G. D. Birla, joined nationalist politics and had great power to design economic policy after independence. The policy was protectionist and hostile to foreign business.

If labour, capital, and managers were difficult to obtain, technology was not. Thanks to the fact that the British Empire enabled free movement of labour, an Indian with money could easily buy machines and hire engineers to run them. Cotton merchants who were frequent visitors to the British textile hubs would be approached by the machinery makers to do this. Over time, the Indian technical personnel learned the work and learned how to repair and recondition machines successfully. The empire enabled similar learning effects in a range of other fields, such as the stationary steam engine, the telegraph, engineering education, and the railways.

Economic historians speculate that the dependence on British standards and equipment delayed domestic engineering education and training. Maybe it did. But we cannot explain something that did not happen. What we do know is that the easy availability of machines and the purchasing power of the merchants made technology more accessible for Indians than it would otherwise be. The educated Indian had a systematic exposure to engineering in factories, canal sites, and railway workshops.

Business and Public Good

Following a long tradition, rich merchants of the nineteenth and twentieth century spent money on charity. The charity was the public forum in which a certain moral code was expressed. According to that code, individual wealth-holders were not owners but trustees of private wealth. Leading merchant families supplied subsistence, cheap credit, and jobs to poorer relations. A lot of organized charity was done by the temples, which were established by the leading merchants. Usually, such charity was a community good, accessible to members of the same caste or sub-caste.[2]

In the 1800s, another model was emerging in the port cities. There was a new priority, education, especially westernized scientific-technical education. Indian merchants, intellectuals, and landholders of Bombay and Calcutta went for western education. When they did, European intellectuals and officers affiliated to the Company administration still believed that the contents of state-sponsored education should be classical Indian learning. Thomas Macaulay discarded this model, but only on a theoretical plane (Chapter 2). In practice, a more effective rejection came from the wealthy Indians who had little patience for European Orientalism.

What was 'western' education? When sponsored or encouraged by the state, education was expected to spread the values of European enlightenment, such as the emergence of humanity from the constraints of religion or tradition. Many Indian students and social reformers saw its value in this way. A secondary purpose was to produce useful knowledge, or workers suitably trained to join commerce, industry, and state service. New schools opened education to all irrespective of caste or status, a model that did not exist before. There was, however, no notion of free education yet. Education could also at the same time become an instrument to command loyalty to colonial rule and impart notions of western superiority. The two sets of values—the desire for freedom and loyalty to foreign rule—would clash. The clash became intense after 1900. In the 1800s, the enlightenment and utilitarian appeal of western knowledge was stronger in the Indian mind.

In the 1810s, four intellectuals and landlords of Calcutta, Radhakanta Deb, Buddhinath Mukherjee, Rasamay Dutt, and Ram Mohan Roy, campaigned successfully for the college that was to become the Presidency College. Interestingly, the most famous names in this set were passionately traditionalist in their own way, but they had no conflict over the aims of modern education. Cowasji Jehangir, Dwarkanath Tagore, and Matilal Seal (Chapter 2) donated money and land to the Calcutta Medical College. In Bombay, the philanthropist and publicist Jagannath Sankarsett, himself from a business family, was instrumental in the establishment of the Elphinstone College (c. 1840). Jamsetjee Jejeebhoy donated money to the Grant Medical College in Bombay (Fig. 3.3). Cowasji Jehangir of the Readymoney family and Premchand Roychand donated to the University of Bombay.

Parsi charity in Bombay began in the same fashion as other merchants. It was, as elsewhere, community-bound. But as Bombay became the principal centre of the community, philanthropy became identified more with public service rather than community service. Money began to move into a variety of non-community institutions, and public institutions such as schools, colleges, hospitals, old-age homes, urban schemes, waterworks, and libraries. For example, Jamsetjee Jejeebhoy's charitable work in the 1850s and the millowner Dinshaw Manakji Petit's in the 1880s followed the old model and consisted of a fund for the relief of poor Parsis, temples, and hospitals. Sir Ratan Tata Trust (1919) and Sir Dorabji Tata Trust (1932), by contrast, represented the new model, the latter defining its mission to promote learning 'without any distinction of place, nationality or creed'. Collectively, the Tata's charities in the twentieth century included the Tata Memorial Cancer Hospital, the Tata Institute of Social Sciences, the Indian Institute of Science, the Tata Institute of Fundamental Research, and Chairs in universities.

Between these dates, several colleges and technical institutes had come up with significant endowments from Parsi merchants and industrialists. Major examples would include the Byramjee Jeejeebhoy Medical College, and several buildings of the Bombay University sponsored by Cowasji Jehangir Readymoney (see above).

Fig. 3.3 Grant Medical College in Bombay. Established in 1845 with a donation from Jamsetjee Jejeebhoy and the Governor of Bombay, Robert Grant, this was one of the first medical colleges in India (© DeGolyer Library, Southern Methodist University, William Johnson Photographs of Western India)

By the end of the century, as the colonial state created a system of self-government in the cities, merchants and industrialists moved into politics quickly. They joined the municipality, port management, famine relief, and general and women's education. For some examples, Gordhandas Khatau, son of Khatau Makanji, was an elected member of the Bombay Corporation; Lalbhai Dalpatbhai, the Ahmedabad mill owner, was an elected member of the Ahmedabad District Board; Sylas Moses, a senior manager of the Sassoon group, was a member of the Bombay Port Trust; George Sutherland, the partner of Begg-Dunlop, was a Sheriff of Calcutta and an elected member of the Bengal legislature.

Any list of influential public intellectuals in the early decades of the twentieth century would contain a number of Parsis, including two Parsi politicians prominent in Britain, Dadabhai Naoroji (1825–1917) and Mancherjee Bhownagree (1851–1933), who were followed by the socialist Shapurji Saklatvala (1874–1936), a pioneer in the trade union movement Sorabji Bengali, a leader of the theosophist movement B. P. Wadia (1881–1958), lawyer and President of the Indian National Congress Pherozeshah Mehta (1845–1915), litterateur, editor and reformer Behramji Malabari (1853–1912), and the nationalist Bhikaji Cama (1861–1936). Ardeshir Shroff, an economist, was an architect of the first development plan.

Artisans

As Chapter 1 showed, the decline of the handicrafts is an iconic episode for Indian economic history scholarship. That there was a decline in employment is certain. It was more serious in generic standardized goods like yarn, iron, or dyes. But since these goods were also raw materials in other artisan industries, like cloth making and metal products, cheaper imports helped those other industries improve productivity. Recent statistical work suggests that the production of hand-spun yarn fell steadily in the nineteenth century to near-zero by 1900 (Fig. 3.4). The production of handwoven cloth fell too until about 1880. It rose thereafter.

The revival of the handloom industry has drawn attention. The attention is justified, for the handicraft industry in general, and handloom weaving of cloth especially was a source of productivity growth in the non-agricultural activities (Fig. 1.1). Cotton handloom weaving engaged about a third of the industrial workforce of 13 million in 1901. Although imported cloth cost much less to buy, consumers preferred hand-woven cloth in some varieties for their quality and craftsmanship. Those weavers that supplied such markets gained from foreign trade. They could access cheaper material, and access new tools and processes. Almost all of the tools and processes adopted by the weavers in late colonial India, such as the fly-shuttle slay, the frame-mounted loom, the jacquard, dobby, drop-box, and synthetic dyes, had been invented in Europe.

These adaptations made the industry stronger but more unequal. Some weavers had grown richer than others by trading in goods and materials, or employing craftsmanship to meet city markets, or adopting

Fig. 3.4 A view of a woman spinning outside a hut, about 1860. A rare photograph of hand-spinning shows the conditions in which the industry carried on: part-time work by women, poverty, and the simplicity of the tools. Mechanized production replaced this type of work easily, which helped the users of cotton yarn but destroyed jobs of poor women (© British Library Board)

new tools. They expanded business and engaged other weavers on wages and on contract. This class of weaver-capitalists set up larger workshops and experimented with new tools.

Artisanal iron production shows the same pattern as the textile industry. In precolonial India, iron ore and charcoal were available in good quantity along the fringes of the Deccan plateau and in some Himalayan regions. However, most such sources of supply were located far away from the cities and the ports, and far away from the consumers of the more complex metal products. Artisan communities producing semi-finished iron tended to be located near the ores and worked on a scale and level of capability adapted to meeting the small rural demand for iron.

In the second half of the nineteenth century, this indigenous smelting declined quickly, when European iron began to come into India on a large scale. The railways reduced transportation costs and brought markets within easy access of the cheaper imported pig iron and steel. Wood fuel began to become scarce, as forests were reserved. Alternative demands for wood in construction, shipbuilding, and railways grew. In some regions, woods ran out.

Meanwhile, imports had created new tastes for iron products. Indians consumed iron in greater quantity and variety than before. In furniture, cutlery, small tools, wood gave way to iron. Cutlery consumption increased, and while it did, local blacksmiths switched over to Swedish and Sheffield steels, strengthening their own craft skills and yet cutting off ties with indigenous smelting. The main beneficiary of imported iron, then, was the urban blacksmith. The specialist blacksmiths understood new consumer markets better than the village smelters. In this sphere, globalization had a more positive effect. Much knowledge was embodied in small tools, which were imported. The city, the ports, the barracks, and the public works allowed unconventional learning opportunities. Indian blacksmiths gained from being there. They worked in mills, started workshops, and joined foundries and forges.

In the same pattern as big business, small business owners too joined politics. The weaver-capitalist-lawyer and leader of the non-Brahmin movement in South India, P. Theagaraya Chetty (1852–1925) was the most famous example.

Conclusion

The growth of trade, industrialization, and revival of the artisan industry together produced the productivity growth that Fig. 1.1 charts. A lot of the impetus was confined to the port cities and their satellites. Factories, railways, banking, even new forms of crafts displayed a city bias. There were three reasons for this. First, they all had a stake in commodity trade which converged in the port city. Second, the cities being more cosmopolitan spaces, skilled people settled down there more readily. Therefore, businesses that needed skilled labour and technology found it easier to obtain them in the big city. Third, the cities offered a better quality of education, which the wealthy wanted to sponsor and valued.

The countryside was dynamic in its own way but made few people really rich. Why?

Notes

1. Tirthankar Roy, 'The Origins of Import Substituting Industrialization in India,' *Economic History of Developing Regions*, 32(1), 2017, 71–95.
2. Tirthankar Roy, *Company of Kinsmen: Community and Enterprise in South Asian History 1700–1950*, Delhi: Oxford University Press, 2010.

Further Reading

D. Bogart and L. Chaudhary, 'Railways in Colonial India: An Economic Achievement?', in L. Chaudhary, B. Gupta, T. Roy and A. Swamy, eds., *A New Economic History of Colonial India*, London: Routledge, 2015.

Douglas Haynes, *Small Town Capitalism in Western India: Artisans, Merchants, and the Making of the Informal Economy, 1870–1960*, Cambridge: Cambridge University Press, 2014.

Tirthankar Roy, *A Business History of India: Enterprise and the Emergence of Capitalism 1700–2015*, Cambridge: Cambridge University Press, 2018.

Tirthankar Roy, *Traditional Industry in the Economy of Colonial India*, Cambridge: Cambridge University Press, 1999.

CHAPTER 4

Unyielding Land

Abstract Although business did well in colonial India, agriculture stayed poor. Cultivation of land engaged more than two-thirds of the employed population. Cultivated land increased by 50% between 1860 and 1920. The opportunity to trade encouraged the trend. That commercialization made many merchants rich. But it made little difference to the peasants and landlords. As population increased, and few people could find good jobs outside the village, the poverty of the village was shared by more people. Why did the village produce more and yet stay poor?

Keywords Agriculture in India · Railways · Commercialization of agriculture in India · Landlords · Moneylenders

Cultivation of land engaged more than two-thirds of the employed population. Cultivated land increased by 50% between 1860 and 1920. The opportunity to trade encouraged the trend. This was a revolution no doubt. It made many merchants rich. Some of them invested their profits in factories and banks. But it made little difference to the peasants and landlords. As population increased, and few people could find good jobs outside the village, the poverty of the village was shared by more people.

Why did the village produce more and yet stay poor?

© The Author(s) 2019

T. Roy, *How British Rule Changed India's Economy*,
Palgrave Studies in Economic History,
https://doi.org/10.1007/978-3-030-17708-9_4

Growth of Trade

Markets and trade in agricultural goods existed on a large scale in the precolonial period. But the market expansion in the nineteenth century was different. There were four differences.

First, before colonial rule, product markets were mainly local, weights and measures varied from place to place, and transportation systems like bullock caravans or river boats were not suitable for trading in bulk over long distances. The railways eased these constraints. Second, India was now part of a global trading order. The Industrial Revolution had Britain specialize in industrial production while buying more food and more raw material from the rest of the world. Export in value from India increased 500% between 1870 and 1914. Non-manufactured goods accounted for 70–80% of the exports. Agricultural prices rose relative to industrial prices. In theory, peasants in the tropics could export the same basket of goods in 1914 as they did in 1870, and yet buy a bigger basket of textiles and metals than in 1870.

Third, responding to these changes, the area cropped increased in most regions. Marketable crops such as wheat, cotton, oilseeds, sugarcane, and tobacco led this process. The fourth change occurred in 'factor' markets. Rents and prices of land, credit transactions, land transfers, and the circulation of agricultural labourers, all increased, though we cannot measure the extent of the rise in all cases. Measures of local transport and rural trade, such as the number of carts at work, show a big rise where such data are available.

After World War I, conditions began to turn adverse. In the 1920s, world agricultural markets faced excess supply. Prices were no longer rising. The agricultural depression was one factor among many that led to the Great Depression in 1929–1932. The Depression upset commodity exports and, by raising the real burden of rural debts, hurt the peasants. Already, good arable land was scarce.

Of the main crops exported, the trade in raw cotton had begun before 1800 and grew in scale from 1870 to 1930. At first, mills in Lancashire found Indian cotton of a quality unsuitable for their machines. When the American Civil War broke out in 1861, supplies of cotton from America stopped abruptly. British factories now devised ways of mixing Indian cotton with other varieties to make it usable. After the war, mills in Bombay emerged as a new market for cotton. Around World War I,

Japan, which had become one of the world's largest textile exporters, also purchased Indian cotton. The Indo-Japanese cotton trade continued until the 1980s.

Indian wheat accounted for 14% of British imports in 1883. Fall in transportation costs and repeal of an export duty on wheat sold from India helped the trade. Rice, by contrast, had a mainly Asian market. Bengal, Burma, and Southeast Asia emerged as the world's main sources of rice. In India, rice formed about a quarter to a third of export in a normal year. Bengal rice went to other Indian provinces and settlements of migrant Indian workers in the empire. The rice eaters among them preferred Bengal rice to the locally grown ones. Famines in any part of monsoon Asia activated these intra-Asian trade flows. For example, in 1863–1865, food shortage in China led to the export of Bengal rice to China. During the Orissa famine (1867–1868), Burma rice was imported into Orissa.

All regions met this increased demand by expanding cultivation. But the scale of the response differed. A key difference was the prospect of irrigation.

The Regions

In a tropical monsoon region, the rainy season can make producing one crop easy, but the rest of the year is dry and sometimes exceedingly hot. The aridity and heat dry up surface water making the cultivation of almost anything difficult unless irrigation in winter or summer permits the production of winter or summer crops. Irrigation was expensive in most parts of the region. The two common modes of irrigation were canals and wells. Canals needed to be taken from perennial rivers, which did not exist except in the deltas and the Indo-Gangetic Basin. Canals could not be constructed with private money because they needed to be built on a large scale. In the Deccan Plateau and central Indian uplands, canals were not easy and groundwater was found too deep to build cheap wells.

In addition to lack of water, much of the Indian subcontinent does not have nutrient-rich loamy soil. In the Indo-Gangetic plains, both soil and water generally offered favourable conditions. But in peninsular India, both soil and water were deficient in quantity or quality, except in the presence of alluvial deposits or the 'regur' soil good for cotton.

When we combine these conditions, it should not surprise that Indian yields were significantly smaller than yields of similar crops in Asia, Europe, and America.

These constraints eased in four regions via large-scale canal building operations. The biggest of these canal systems came up in Punjab. Before 1850, Punjab was an arid area containing a vast savannah that supported pastoralism but little cultivation. Monsoon rains died away in the western part of the region, and intensive cultivation was possible only close to rivers, or in narrow strips watered by wells. The region, however, had large perennial rivers formed in the Himalayas. In the 1840s, engineering projects were a business of the army. In 1848–1849, a group of army officers and engineers stationed in Punjab during a military campaign observed that a canal network was possible in this open space. Proby Cautley, the architect of the Ganges canal (below), was their inspiration. When the last major battle in Anglo-Sikh wars, Chilianwala, was over, Lieutenant R. Baird-Smith who had experience with canals wrote a pamphlet about 'opening up' Punjab to British commerce and doubling the revenue of the province. Canals would be the stone that killed the two birds. The report was precise on the feasibility of controlling and rechanneling the flow of river water.

Between 1870 and 1920, engineers built canals tapping the waters of the five rivers of Punjab, turning the interfluvial tracts, which earlier sustained only pastoralism, into arable land. Nine 'canal colonies' created out of these irrigation projects appeared. The projects irrigated five million acres. The earliest colony was Sidhnai, and the last the Nili Bar. The largest were Lower Chenab (two million acres), Lower Bari Doab and Nili Bar (a million acres each).

In these colonies, the available land was distributed to claimants in lots of 14–50 acres each. In allotting these grants, the government favoured claimants of peasant background. Special considerations were made for families with a record of service to British rule, including service in the army. That policy made Punjab a major recruiting ground for the army. Until 1912, the land grantees were technically tenants of the state, a situation they accepted reluctantly. The Colonization Act of 1912 allowed them to become proprietors. If the entire scheme wanted to secure the loyalty of the peasantry to British rule, it succeeded in that aim. Punjab peasants were loyal to the rule in the 1930s when peasants elsewhere joined the nationalist movement.

Between 1867 and 1921, not only did the length of canals increase from less than 2000 miles to more than 15,000 miles, but also road length nearly doubled, and railway mileage grew fourfold. The combined revolution raised output, cultivated area, trade, revenue. After 1921, the conversion of wastes reached its limits, but plant breeding experiments in wheat and cotton bore results.

A second vanguard region was formed of the two South Indian deltas, Godavari and Krishna, where canals came up in the 1840s, encouraging rice cultivation and trade and the business of the local ports. The canals also encouraged diversification into the profitable oilseeds, sugarcane, tobacco, turmeric, chilly and plantains and stimulated small-scale industry such as oil, rice, tobacco, and sugar factories. These activities were concentrated in towns that grew in population and economic importance, like Vijayawada, Eluru, Rajahmundry, and Vizagapatam. The bulk of India's tobacco crop came to be grown in the nearby Guntur district.

A third vanguard region was the present-day western Uttar Pradesh (UP) and Haryana states, where a network of canals (later called Ganges and Jumna) was constructed in the nineteenth century. This network used in part disused channels created by the Indo-Islamic states that had ruled the region from the fourteenth century. Unlike Punjab, UP was not water-scarce. Here, the canals made water cheaper and encouraged growing water-intensive cash crops like sugarcane. The railway network was denser in the Gangetic plains and encouraged regional specialization. The canal belts produced the more lucrative wheat and sugarcane, and poorer areas in the periphery (like Bundelkhand) switched to cheaper grains. Agents of European grain-trading companies set up branches in the main towns at the intersection of railways, roads, and river routes.

The fourth area to receive canal water was Sind. Sind is proverbially a gift of the Indus, containing a vast alluvial plain watered by the river and several other manmade or natural channels. Although the larger region received little rainfall and had to live with extreme heat, a big tract in southern Sindh or *Lar* was regularly inundated by the rising water of the Indus. The alluvium and the organic substance the floods left behind, made these lands exceedingly fertile, giving rise to three crops in a year, and some of the highest yields of rice known in South Asia. Sind also had a network of state canals. After the British assumed power in 1842, a Canal and Forest Department looked after this network. The department decided that a dam at the Sukkur gorge would be a good idea. The

Sukkur barrage took a century to become operational. But canal construction was not neglected. Thus, the cultivated area expanded from 1.4 million acres in 1885 to 3.9 million acres in 1925. Karachi emerged as a major seaport. With customs reforms on the western border, the extension of the Indus steamboat business, and a railway line that connected Karachi with Lahore, Sind saw a revolution like Punjab.

Dramatic as some of these stories are, the average situation was not rosy at all. A change did come but was confined to a few crops and a few areas, and almost never accompanied by a rise in land yield (Table 4.1). Much of peninsular India is located on the Deccan Plateau. Poor soil and unreliable rainfall had made most of the Deccan a millet-growing region doing subsistence agriculture. The black soil zones in Deccan, however, were suitable for the cultivation of cotton. Cotton cultivation and trade had been growing slowly in this region through the first half of the nineteenth century. The railways stimulated the trade. In the same broad area, a few pockets of canal irrigation did appear. One of these was a network of canals in the Nira river valley south of Poona built as a famine protection measure. The project attracted migrant farmers from outside the region and emerged as a concentration of sugar manufacturing.

In the East, the alluvial flat of the Ganges delta (much of this land is presently located in Bangladesh), was already densely populated and did not see major changes in crops, yield, and area. As the population of Bengal increased, so did the pressure on land. Much of central India consisted of forested lands that did not sustain profitable agriculture and was inaccessible by the railways and roads. With one or two exceptions, the region remained agriculturally poor.

Table 4.1 Agricultural production, land area, productivity (annual percentage growth rate, British India, 1891–1946)

	Production	*Land area*	*Productivity (yield/hectare)*
All crops	0.37	0.37	0.01
Food crops	0.11	0.31	–0.18
Other crops	1.31	0.42	0.67

Source George Blyn, *Agricultural Trends in India*, Philadelphia: University of Pennsylvania, 1967, Appendix Table 5A

Berar and Narmada Valley were two exceptions in the otherwise bleak central India. The Narmada Valley had a special irrigation system. Rainwater was trapped on the land by constructing banks to increase the moisture of the soil in the drier months. In some cases, a rice crop was grown in this water just before the wheat sowing season. Berar was good for cotton. Major railway lines connecting these areas with Bombay, Calcutta, and northern India encouraged exports.

With such a mixed picture as this one, how did the rural classes fare on average?

Peasants and Landlords

Real income in agriculture increased at roughly 1–2% per head in 1860–1914, somewhat faster than did real wage. In the vanguard regions, peasants became richer. Everywhere else, the group that gained was small in relation to the set that did not.

What conditions made the gainers distinct from the rest? They were peasants with enough land to be able to sell grain or cotton after meeting their own needs. In the ryotwari areas, they owned land. In zamindari regions, they were the dominant tenant farmers whom the landlords (zamindars) depended on and made friends with. The rising peasants also owned or controlled credit, water, tools, and animals. These groups organized themselves in caste collectives, using caste as a political bargaining platform. The Jat peasantry in Punjab and Upper Doab (Fig. 4.1), the Vellalas in Tamil Nadu, the jotedars or tenants with occupancy rights in Bengal, the Kanbi Patidars of south Gujarat, the Reddy farmers in Madras-Deccan, the Maratha peasants and Saswad Malis in the Maharashtra sugarcane belt, illustrate the process.

At the lower end, opportunities for improvement were limited. Peasants with small holdings suffered during famines and slumps. The famines impoverished them and reduced the supply of working males. Small peasants had to live with insecurity of tenancy, high risk of cultivation, and limited capital resources.

Since the latter type was more numerous, the average income of the peasant was small, which should explain why peasants from overpopulated and arid areas migrated to off-season urban work (Chapter 3). Because of the high seasonality of monsoon agriculture, there was seasonal unemployment even among the better off peasants. Agriculture rarely offered full-time work for more than 220–240 days in a year, in

Fig. 4.1 Jat landholders, about 1890. This illustration of a group of cultivators from northern India is one example of a set of photographs made of occupational groups for circulation in Britain (© IndiaPicture/Alamy Stock Photo)

the dry regions much less than that. Even when wages in the factories, mines and plantation estates were only marginally higher than what a peasant expected to earn in agriculture, there was more work available in factories, mines, and plantations. Even the well off peasant families tried to send their adult males off to wage-work, recalling them to meet the peak season workload.

Despite poverty, the poor held on to land even when they worked harder to make the same amount of money as before. For one thing, the majority of the rural people would not either find jobs in the cities or enter them easily with the skills they had. Besides, Chapter 2 showed that new laws were expected to make land more saleable, but in practice did not. There was some sale no doubt. In the ryotwari areas, peasants mortgaged their land more frequently than before and often had to sell if they were unable to repay loans. In northern and southern India, former military and priestly groups, who owned land but did not cultivate with their own hands, sometimes sold land to join other professions. But overall, land was sold and resold to a small extent. Only 1–2% of landholding changed hands over several decades. Peasants held on to land for the little security it gave them. The accent on joint family and kinship in the law of land ownership made land poorly marketable. And debt legislation restrained the ability of the moneylenders to take over land (see below).

How did the landlords fare? In the zamindari areas, all peasants were technically tenants without ownership rights. Initially, there was no law protecting tenants. This imbalance empowered the zamindar. Some zamindars used their power to exploit the weaker peasants, usually with the help of dominant peasants. Some zamindars in the south-eastern coastal areas lived like mini kings in their estates. But this imbalance did not last long.

In Bengal, tenancy acts (1859–1928) recognized and strengthened the occupancy rights of peasants settled on a piece of land for many generations. In other regions too, tenancy protection was a general trend. Occupancy right could make the occupancy tenant something like a small-scale landlord and encourage a sublease market. Tenancy regulation tried to keep up with this trend, but never quite managed to do so. Money rents increased manifold between the early twentieth century and mid-twentieth century in North India and a few other regions. And yet, the rent the zamindar of Bengal could collect was fixed by law. This anomaly empowered the richer tenants. Zamindars did not prosper after the restrictions came in, and most suffered a steady loss of economic and political power from the late nineteenth century.

Pressed for money, the zamindars whose estates contained forest lands, started destroying forests to expand cultivation. When this process was in full swing, a young Bengali gentleman with a flair for writing took up a job as a manager in a north Bihar estate. This was Purneah district in north Bihar, the least populated district of the province in the 1890s. This gentleman loved the forest, but his duty was to destroy it. His memoirs of those years, a classic autobiographical work in the Bengali language, presents possibly the best first-hand account of the crisis in the estates, destruction of zamindari forest and the dilemma it posed to the environmentalist of the time.[1]

The Wage-Labourer

The censuses show that the extent of wage labour increased in colonial times. Marxist historians said that new property rights in land, a decline of the handicrafts, high risks of cultivation, and peasant indebtedness, forced small peasants to become wage labourers. A different reading said that older forms of landlessness associated with caste gave way to a new form associated with wage-work.[2] The census was able to observe wage labour better than traditional bonded labour and exaggerated the change.

Besides, more women than men became wage-dependent. The disparity shows that whereas those who lost a traditional livelihood in the crafts could migrate to urban work, the men did so more readily. Rural women were less likely to move to the cities because they married early and had children to look after. The women who stayed behind reported themselves to the census as agricultural workers, because that was the work they usually did against payment of money.

I mentioned caste-based bondage. What was this? Slavery and serfdom were rare in India. The closest equivalent of serfdom was a caste-based obligation to perform labour, and prohibition on some lower castes from ownership of land. In Kerala, individuals so tied to land were in effect sold when the land was sold. A more common form of labour-tying was the farm servant contract when the male head of a family pledged his labour, sometimes his family's labour, for several years to one employer. While caste sometimes cemented these relationships, there was an insurance motive behind the arrangement. The timing of rainfall was a life and death matter for peasants in monsoon agriculture. For many employers, it was well worth paying subsistence to a person throughout the year against assured supply of work on the few days when sowing and harvesting must be done. The average duration of such employment contracts was in decline from the late nineteenth century. The percentage of farm servants in agricultural labour households was falling everywhere. In Madras, where farm servant contracts were particularly prevalent, the fall was dramatic. An increasing supply of migrants reduced the employers' need for hoarding labour in this way.

Despite the increasing demand for wage labour, wages did not rise much. There were episodes of rising real wage (such as in Punjab), but these were exceptional. In the long run, real wage stayed stable. Only the number of people who earned this stable and low wage increased. Between 1881 and 1931, the proportion of landless labourers in agriculture increased from 15% of the workforce to 20%. They numbered 15 million in 1881, 20 in 1931 (and more than 100 million in 2001 in the Indian Union alone). Why did the number increase?

The fall in tied labour increased the supply and circulation of workers willing to work for a market wage. There was another reason. The cultivated land area grew slowly from the second decade of the twentieth century, whereas population increased faster than before. The old land was already owned, so the additional population must live either by dividing old plots, which would push them towards tenancy and labour. But population pressure would not alone explain the real wage stagnation if yield could rise. The truth is, yield did not rise. Real wage in agriculture followed trends in labour productivity closely. This was low and unchanging. As the population grew, more people of small means needed to earn extra money from doing labour on the side.

Social status sometimes added its weight to suppress wage growth. In precolonial India, landless labourers came from those castes whose primary duty was to perform agricultural labour. It was not easy to escape these obligations while an individual worker remained in the same village. Access to land continued to be caste-biased. With some exceptions, the wealthier people in the countryside came from the middle or upper castes, whereas the poor tended to come from castes that had performed labour for generations. Economic inequality strengthened social inequality and vice versa.

Still, many labourers did escape the brutality of the village. Farm servant contract and caste-based servitude did decline. From the early twentieth century, there was an improvement in the social status of the depressed castes. The element of compulsion and force in their employment became weaker. Various forms of social oppression, such as enforced dress codes and codes of conduct with respect to upper castes, became weaker too. The government, where it could, took the side of the oppressed people, resisting local community pressure. The possibility of migrating to the cities and to other British colonies made the occupational choice more diverse. The decline of tied labour was partly a result of the exit of these castes from agricultural labour, as these people entered plantations, mines, urban services, public works, and government utilities.

Moneylenders

There was huge growth in rural credit, as one would expect in a commercializing economy. The decision to produce non-food crops meant that the peasant had to borrow to buy food from the market. Rent and tax payments required taking loans, especially if the timing of these payments occurred before the harvest. Storage and transport of cash crops required money. Sugarcane, cotton, and tobacco required water and fertilizer, and investment in land preparation. The cotton crop on black soil needed heavy ploughs and many bullocks. These crops remained on the field longer than most foodgrains and thus required a longer waiting period between investment and sale of the crop.

On the supply side, the creation of property rights in land, and investment in water enhanced the mortgage value of land. The railways, growth of market towns, and new profit opportunities increased the mobility, migration, settlement, and enterprise of persons of trader-moneylender castes. Legislation on credit contracts gave the creditors more power to recover loans.

Paradoxically, all this change caused more anxiety than celebration among officers.

The Colonist Model of Poverty: The Evil Lender

Chapter 1 mentioned that the British defenders of the empire were on the backfoot when they were asked: If British India was a beneficial rule why did the village suffer so much from poverty and famines? They invented a fiction to answer this question.

Administrators believed that the peasants were taking loans by mortgaging their property to the moneylender and were at risk of losing land. In Poona and Ahmednagar districts in the summer of 1875, peasant mobs raided and burnt a few houses belonging to Gujarati and Marwari moneylenders. With the memory of the Mutiny still fresh in their minds, officials panicked. The long-term effect of their fear was the Deccan Agricultural Relief Act (1879), which restrained moneylender activity, land sales, and the credit market. The Act set off a chain reaction. In Punjab, the canal colonies had given a big push to credit. Officials felt that the control of professional moneylenders over rural assets was increasing to the detriment of the peasantry. The Punjab Land Alienation Act (1900–1901) followed, to again restrain mortgage and transfers.

The Deccan Riots were a minor event, in Punjab, there was no crisis at all. But the authorities needed a scapegoat, for famines and peasant unrest shook up their fundamental belief. The British in India proudly believed that they looked after the interests of the peasants, and played the part of 'an improving proprietor on an enormous scale'.[3] 'The Government of India', wrote Lord Mayo (Viceroy 1867–1872), '.. is the chief landlord. The duties which in England are performed by a good landlord fall in India .. upon the Government'. If the government played its part well, and there was no doubt in its own mind that it did, why were the peasants poor and restless?

The narrative of the evil lender answered the question. Elements of that narrative can be found scattered in writings, speeches, and reports, such as the Punjab officer S. S. Thorburn's writings on moneylenders, the Scottish agriculturist and writer James Caird's note of dissent submitted to the Indian Famine Commission (1880), and Viceroy and poet Robert Bulwer-Lytton's impassioned defence of the Deccan debt relief act before the British Parliament. The theory said that the peasants were poor and restless because the exploitative moneylenders had taken advantage of modern contract laws, and squeezed the poor dry more efficiently than in earlier regimes.

Lytton (Viceroy 1876–1880) made the case for a Deccan moneylending act with a dubious flourish of rhetoric: 'is it not obvious that if in any part of India the actual cultivators of the soil see .. their personal freedom .. passing from them into the hands of a class whom .. they regard as the authors of their ruin .. under the protection of laws which .. they regard as the engines of it, the bitterness of sentiment .. must be a chronic incentive .. to social disturbances?'[4] The so-called Punjab school of administration, pro-peasant on all matters, held a definite view about why the government needed to step in to restrain the moneylender. 'In some sense we govern India,' wrote Thorburn, 'chiefly to their [merchants' and moneylenders'] advantage'.[5] And therefore, the government was 'jeopardising the stability of our hold on the affections of the people, ..[by] helping petty shop-keepers and money-lenders to exploit the country for their own benefit'.

British rule in India and its laws, the myth said, had strengthened the hands of the creditor over that of the debtor, if not by design. The time had come to reverse this bias. As the title of Thorburn's book (*Musalmans and Moneylenders*) shows, officers saw inequality in communal terms, the peasants being poor Muslims and the moneylenders rich Hindus, thus starting a narrative that bore bitter fruit in the communal riots of the 1940s. Significantly, all of these statements date roughly to the decade after the Deccan famine of 1876–1878, a time when the imperialists had gone seriously on the defensive.

Driven by the image of the evil moneylender, the state passed laws to prohibit land rights passing on to the creditor and effectively neutralized the moneylenders if not removed them from the scene. That image became an enduring legacy of the colonist model of poverty. The image stuck in policy-making. In India after independence, economists inherited this legacy to ruthlessly persecute the moneylender. From theory, it became a sentiment. The image of evil moneylender inspired countless popular cinema and fiction, including the Bollywood classic *Mother India*. In the 1970s, Marxist historians revived the idea and built theories of rural poverty using the image of the evil moneylender, not realizing how passive and imperialist their thinking was.

The sentiment did not help the peasant. As recent work by Latika Chaudhary and Anand Swamy shows, the anti-moneylending laws reduced the supply of credit (kept interest rates high) and pushed the credit underground in a sense. The business shifted from the professional moneylender to the rich peasant. The rich and middle peasants tied credit with the sale (that is, collected an implicit interest from commodity prices, something a moneylender could not do). This was a more exploitative arrangement than an open credit business with suitable regulation.

In 1973, the economist Amit Bhaduri suggested that economic power based on property and capital could cause agricultural backwardness. With the Bengal landlords in mind, the theory says that those who owned land could earn easy money by exploiting tenants and labourers, and they took this easy road. They neglected the harder road of making productive investments and earn profits instead. Following models like these that hold property rights accountable, some economists think that the zamindar was the villain of the countryside. They oversimplify history. Historians who have studied zamindars have shown how their economic power was in decline from the mid-1800s. Zamindari rent was regulated by law from 1859, the price of rice rose by 200% in the next 70 years, so that their real income must have fallen to a third of what it was in the early-1800s. The evil zamindar is as much a myth as the evil lender.

Most such theories that blame property right for rural poverty can be shown to be simplistic and flawed. The lender took a great deal of risk to do the business. The regulatory laws made things harder for them. There is plenty of evidence that landowners readily invested in land improvement if they could foresee profits to be made from that decision. If they did not, the decision would mean that there was not much profit to be made. Most property-right-based theories apply to specific regions, whereas the problem of low and stagnant yield was universal.

We need a better theory of stagnation of yield and underinvestment.

Another Theory: Limited Resource and High Risk

Chapter 3 showed that business firms invested money using trading profits, even when the capital markets were missing. Why could the peasants not use their profits to invest in land improvement? Obviously, either profits were low or the risks were high.

Peasant poverty came in two forms. Parts of the Indo-Gangetic Basin had good land and plenty of water, but a small land–man ratio. And the arid regions in peninsular India (see Map 4.1) had too little good land with access to water. In both situations, capital was in short supply. In the overpopulated areas, the land produced a lot but average landholding was too small. In Bengal, Bihar or eastern UP income from rice was shared between too many people dependent on land. The land yield

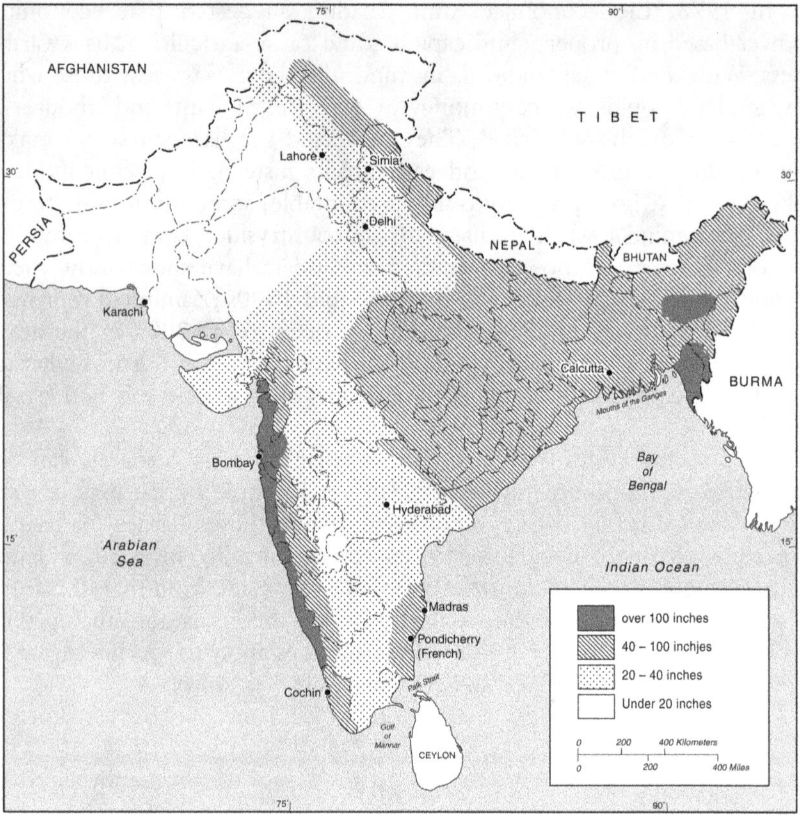

Map 4.1 Rainfall

was above the Indian average, but the number of families dependent on wages and insecure tenancy was growing. Most such people would have no chance of borrowing money for long-term investment in land improvement because the lenders found safer investment opportunities outside agriculture. The zamindars shared their growing poverty, and were not the cause of it.

Much of India remained rain-fed at the end of colonial rule (rain-fed = without manmade irrigation, see irrigation proportions in Table 4.2). In the rain-fed arid lands, good land and water were scarce.

Table 4.2 Irrigated area as a proportion of cultivated area 1885–1938 (%)

	1885–1886	*1938–1939*	*% increase in irrigated area due to government canals*
Punjab	29.3	57.4	95.5
Madras	24.1	23.5	49.6
United Provinces	19.3	26.6	57.0
Rest of British India	6.0	12.5	31.3

Source Statistical Abstracts for British India, various years

Expected earnings from investment in the land were low. In the arid Deccan plateau, conditions for canal irrigation were poor. Sinking wells was the only reliable way to ensure two or three good crops in a year. The low water table in the uplands, the thin topsoil, the scarcity of perennial rivers and the basaltic rock underneath, made digging wells or constructing canals prohibitively expensive and with a high chance of failure. The main grains in these areas were a locally consumed arid area crop, millets, which gave a small profit in the best of seasons.

Conclusion

There was a big growth in the cultivated land area in 1860–1940, to meet the demand for food and material. Whereas the merchants gained from this process, the peasants gained only when assured water, access to the railways, and command over enough land, came together. Take away one of these conditions, and peasants not only did not gain much but were exposed to the risk of losing in a famine all that they had. Only a few peasants in a few regions met all three conditions. These regions I have called vanguards. The situation elsewhere was either there was little water and good soil, or too many people shared the benefits of water and good soil.

After 1920, there was no more land left to exploit, and the extension of cultivation came to a stop. The yield was small and constant. The countryside fell deeper into poverty. Further bursts of output expansion had to await the Green Revolution of the 1970s.

Could the government change the condition that kept the village poor?

Notes

1. Bibhutibhushan Bandopadhyay, *Aranyak* (serialized 1937–1939, events refer to the 1920s).
2. Dharma Kumar, *Land and Caste in South India: Agricultural Labour in Madras Presidency in the Nineteenth Century*, Cambridge: Cambridge University Press, 1965.
3. William Hunter cited in P. J. Thomas, *The Growth of Federal Finance in India*, London: Humphrey Milford, 1939, 7.
4. S. S. Thorburn, *Musalmans and Money-Lenders in the Punjab*, Edinburgh and London: William Blackwood, 1886, 40.
5. Thorburn, *Musalmans and Money-Lenders*, 45.

Further Reading

Latika Chaudhary, et al., 'Agriculture,' in L. Chaudhary, B. Gupta, T. Roy, and A. Swamy, eds., *A New Economic History of Colonial India*, London: Routledge, 2015.

Tirthankar Roy, 'A Delayed Revolution: Environment and Agrarian Change in India,' *Oxford Review of Economic Policy*, 23(2), 2007, 239–250.

CHAPTER 5

A Poor State

Abstract One of the duties of the state in a poor country should be to help raise the productivity of the poorest earners. The poorest earners were the peasants, the agricultural workers, oppressed castes, and the women among these groups. In many respects, the Raj had a more modern form of government than previous Indian regimes. But it spent little on those heads that would make a real difference to the poorest earners. Why did it fail in this duty?

Keywords India Office · Public debt · Drain theory · Gold Exchange Standard · Tariffs

What should a government in a poor country do? Surely, one of the things it should do is help to raise the productivity of the poorest earners? Chapter 4 showed what jobs the poorest people did. This chapter shows that the state did little to raise productivity in these jobs. Before we get too judgemental, we should note that this was an enormously difficult challenge, one that the post-independence Indian state was not too successful in dealing with. But the small capacity of the colonial state did not help matters either.

In many respects, British India had a more modern form of government than previous Indian regimes. It had a more diversified revenue base than the Mughals or the states succeeding the Mughals. It spent less

© The Author(s) 2019

T. Roy, *How British Rule Changed India's Economy*,
Palgrave Studies in Economic History,
https://doi.org/10.1007/978-3-030-17708-9_5

on luxuries and more on the genuine duties of the state such as defence, welfare, infrastructure, and institutions. Yet, it spent far too little on those heads that would make a real difference to the poorest earners. It did little to help raise agricultural productivity. At the top level, the administration lacked ideas about developing India. When a discussion finally began, in the 1920s, the government was going bankrupt.

Economic historians sometimes study the effects of colonial rules by first assuming the purpose of the rule and then assuming the effects. Following that approach, they have invented a menu of words like 'predatory', 'laissez-faire', 'liberal', 'night-watchman', and 'extractive' to describe British India. This is a futile play with rhetoric. These words smuggle in two assumptions that are wrong. First, we can be sure what the intentions of the rulers really were. In fact, the colonial state did not leave any evidence on what it wanted. It did not work to a definite plan. It did desire to keep markets open, but that aim many countries in the nineteenth century shared. And second, the rulers had the capacity to make a change but did not make the change because they did not want to. In fact, the capacity was small, but I will show that it was small partly because India was a colony.

Let me start with that point, and ask, what made colonialism colonial, that is, deliver a weak state?

What Made a Colonial Government Colonial?

The answer to the question is multiple heads of government. This was a government with three heads. After 1858, the India Office in London managed currency, kept reserves and raised loans from London banks. During much of its career, the Office performed currency management well enough, making rupee a stable currency and India government securities acceptable abroad. To do this, it needed to be careful about meeting the government's payment obligations abroad. In India, the Governor-General or Viceroy collected the Indian taxes and made the budget. The Viceroy decided policy in consultation with a Council, consisting of members who specialized in law, military affairs, and public works. The third head of the government was the provinces where the local government raised some local taxes and spent this money and what it received from the centre on roads, schools, and hospitals.

These three levels did not work in concert. Their priorities were different. Trade, exchange, and defence were of great importance to

London. The viceroy seated in Calcutta was more concerned with the public finances. Local welfare engaged the provinces. When British and Indian interests seemed to conflict, these three levels at times took different views. In the nineteenth century, the India Office won some major battles. But the balance tilted in favour of India in the twentieth century. This discord was at the heart of Indian policy-making.

This division of duties was useful for some purposes, such as raising loans in London. But it made innovation and experiments in expenditure policy more difficult. As a result, the government stayed perpetually poor. Tax and loans in national income formed a low 3–5% throughout. Tax per head in British India was among the smallest in the world. It was small even within the empire.[1] This small state spent a considerable part of its income on the army and was unable and unwilling to spend money on infrastructure and welfare. Divided-heads was a disaster in the 1930s when India needed to pursue a more autonomous currency policy from Britain's.

Why was the state so poor to begin with?

Funding the State

State revenues came mainly from land taxes in the nineteenth century. Land revenue, given the generally poor yield of land, was low per head and per acre. After the Mutiny, there was no stomach for squeezing the peasant to raise more money. The dependence on an archaic land tax reduced. But newer and more modern taxes were slow to develop.

Land revenue accounted for 80–95% of total revenue in 1809–1810. In 1858–1859, land tax yielded about half of total revenues. Provincial statistics show quite a large variation in the pattern. The Permanent Settlement areas show the least dependence on land revenue because the nominal amount of tax was fixed forever in 1793, and the real value of that money had fallen to almost nothing by 1900. Next in importance were two commodity taxes of a rather special nature. One was levied on the export of opium, and the other on the sale of salt. Together, the taxes on these two items accounted for 24% of revenues in 1858–1859. The more modern type of taxes such as the income tax, customs, and excise formed a small proportion (12% in 1858–1859).

After World War I, the pattern of taxation changed. The importance of land tax decreased to about 20% of revenue in the 1920s. Land tax as a proportion of the value of agricultural production declined from possibly 10% of net output in the middle or early nineteenth century to less than five in the 1930s. The opium and salt taxes were also a smaller source than before. Opium had become politically incorrect, the salt tax was unfair on the poor, and land tax was too dangerous to play with.

On the other hand, scarcity of money forced the government to experiment with customs and income tax. In this effort, the government could score some success only in the interwar period. Until then, British exporters lobbied hard against protection within the empire. As their influence fell in the interwar period, import tariffs could rise. Income tax again was the scene of a battle. The government did not have the machinery to implement a tax on self-employed people. The groups that could be more easily targeted and assessed were those closest to the government. These were the government employees, and owners of industrial companies, many of whom were Europeans. In 1913–1914, of the total income tax collected, nearly half came from government officers earning high salaries. Of the rest, 75% was contributed by merchants, 8% by services such as lawyers and doctors, 10% by property owners, and 3% by industry. Calculating the taxable income of merchants was a difficult matter because the merchants refused to disclose accounts, the officers could not read and understand what was shown them, and the assets of the firms did not give a full picture of their income. Because of these problems, the success in raising money was modest at best.

The limited revenue was spent on defence, civil administration, and debt service. British India was not a militarily weak state. It spent enough to maintain a large army. By this means, British India kept the princely states pacified, and the internal and external borders open to trade, migration, and investment. The military power of British India was an instrument to forge integration between the Indian economy and the world economy, and to forge closer integration of markets within South Asia. If, after Adam Smith, integrated and smoother market exchange is a condition for development, British India created that condition. But there was a price for this. The state never had much money left over to spend on public good or agricultural development.

Some of the expenditures on defence and administration were made in sterling and went out of the country. This payment by the government was known as the Home Charges. For example, interest payment on loans raised to finance construction of railways and irrigation works, pensions paid to retired officers, and purchase of stores, were payments in sterling. Home Charges were, then and later, controversial and led to the drain theory of Indian poverty.

Drain: A Word Posing as a Theory

From the time when Dadabhai Naoroji (Chapter 1) first made the argument, critics of colonial rule have insisted that any form of payment in foreign currency was a symbol of India's colonial status, a forced extraction or tribute, and harmed India while helping Britain. Ordinarily, India maintained an export surplus and purchased services abroad with the surplus. All service purchases were the target of this attack. To the question—what was colonial about this colonial state?—the drain theorists answered, purchase of services from Britain.

The answer built upon a confused economic reasoning. The drain should mean a payment without adequate return. India did make a payment without adequate return between 1757/1765 and 1772/1784 when a coterie of officers of the East India Company had access to the tax resources of Bengal and used it to buy textiles for export. The actual scale of the transaction cannot be fully known because exactly how much money the Company could grab cannot be accurately estimated. In principle, the Company had a share of the Bengal revenue. But the ruling Nawab had a share too. The division is not clear. Around 1763, the total state revenue of Bengal was £3 million, The Company's export from Bengal was 13% of this at £0.38 million. The major part of the revenue was not used for trade but for the military, administrative, and some infrastructure expenditure. By 1772, Parliamentary regulation ended the conflict of interest (mercantile and political). The Company was no longer in sole charge of ruling Bengal.

After this point, almost all money that the government paid abroad corresponded to the purchase of a service from abroad. Were all these payments without return? The drain theorists imply that they were. By liberally using the word 'tribute' they make it seem as if all payment for services was payment without return. Calculations of the drain are not worth the ink they are written with. Simon Digby thought £1000 million was transferred between 1757 and 1815. Angus Maddison reduced this to £100 million. Javier Cuenca Esteban placed the figure closer to £40 million.[2] If we take the third figure, the implied annual transfer against an estimated national income (1800) of £100–150 million is trivial.

The balance of payments system that emerged after 1800 was based on standard business principles. India bought something and paid for it. State revenues were used to pay for wages of people hired abroad, pay for interest on loans raised abroad, and repatriation of profits on foreign investments coming into India. These were legitimate market transactions. Some overpayment was embedded in these transactions, but no one can tell how big that was.

Indian nationalists brushed off the difficulty by suggesting that all of the export surplus was forced and a waste of money.[3] The crudeness of the claim beggars belief. The architect of the drain theory, for example, abused foreign investment in a language that would put hardcore leftists to shame. 'Foreign capital,' he thundered, 'does nearly all the work, and carries away all the profit. Foreign capitalists .. make profits from the resources of British India, and take away those profits to their own countries.'[4] He alleged that the charge on account of the British Indian army or the marine fleet was unproductive because it was sometimes deployed for purposes other than the defence of Indian waters. However, the fleet also normally guarded trade routes. For the Indian merchant diaspora whose business interests were spread over Africa, Southeast Asia, and East Asia, the defence of their interests did not mean only the defence of a border drawn on land. The British public, which on average paid ten times more than their Indian counterparts towards the maintenance of the fleet subsidized the security of Indian capitalists abroad.[5]

The target of Naoroji's fiercest attack, interest on public debt shows the muddled thinking clearly. Because the tax base was weak and yet the government was creditworthy, the only way the British Indian state could possibly fund its capital expenditure in India was by raising loans in London. The Indian capital market was prohibitively expensive. The most economical option was to raise loans in the cheapest market in the world, London. Naoroji reserved for his harshest attack the only sensible way to fund development in India. If the loans were sourced from India, India's taxpaying peasants would be much poorer than they were.

The premise on which the drain idea was based was that services purchased from abroad were necessarily a waste of money. In the nineteenth century, a lot of payments were made for services that India needed but could not supply on its own. After all, the two countries were worlds apart in their technical-scientific and managerial capabilities. In 1900, foreign labour and foreign capital were employed in modern industry, banks, and trading firms. Firms needed to get these resources from abroad because many types of skilled labour were unavailable in India.

Although the drain theory of poverty is a confused claptrap, the sentiment behind the drain deserves understanding. The aspiring Indian middle classes in the early twentieth century developed a resentment over the fact that less talented and less competent British officers were promoted over the heads of Indian officers, earned more money for less work, and had the top jobs reserved for them. Government appointments policy had built into it a growing paranoia bordering on racism with respect to the educated Indians. The resentment is understandable, and the recruitment policy to the top jobs was both unfair and wasteful.

But the government itself formed a tiny part of the economic system, so the potential waste was of small order. At present, top jobs in government earn a salary that is about 20 times the per capita income. In 1870, top jobs in government earned about 100 times the per capita income. Such salaries went to about 6000 officers. The combined overpayment should amount to 0.03% of national income.

The government did have serious failing. Its real failing was not what it did with the money it earned, but that it did not try harder to earn more and to spend more.

Not Enough Capital

Ordinarily, about a quarter of total expenditure went to the construction and repair of national assets. The percentage of public investment in expenditure fell quickly towards the end of the interwar period, as debt service and administrative commitments took priority over investment.

There was a positive correlation between capital raised abroad, whether directly through public debt or indirectly by railway companies whose profits the state guaranteed, and capital investment. Funds raised in this way went to finance irrigation, roads, railways, and telegraphs. Increasingly from the interwar period, investments under these heads went into repair rather than the creation of new assets.

Schools and hospitals, however, were funded from the budget. In the twentieth century, there was more demand for social spending, which came from a sense that education was a means of social advancement that the colonial rulers had neglected. Partly, political decentralization after 1919, when provincial budgets became more exposed to local political pressures, added to the demand. High levels of illiteracy and mortality showed that being a colony of Britain for over half a century had done little to enable India to approach British standards of social development. A slight rise in the proportion of public spending on education and health in the interwar period reflects an attempt to redress this neglect of social infrastructure.

There was an acute shortage of money to do this, and as I have shown, success in diversifying the revenue base was small. A big puzzle is that the British Indian government had access to the cheapest and most developed money market in the world, that British Indian debt was rated high in this market, and yet, the government seemed conservative about raising debt and using it to expand its developmental activities. Debt-GDP ratio was low (around 15–20% in the late nineteenth century), and rose up to about 25 in 1880, but from that point onward started falling. It rose again in the 1930s, but this was an effect of fall in national income. In sources on public finance, there is no clear explanation of why the government was so cautious about raising money in London when it was easy to do so.

One answer is, raising more debt in London would mean higher payment by the Indian Government abroad on account of debt service, this the Indian nationalists did not accept. They attacked interest on the public debt as the most onerous type of drain.[6] The British in India were afraid both of Indian opinion as they were of British public opinion. A second problem was that the divided-heads syndrome kept the financial policy conservative. The Government of India might decide something to be important, but it did not have control over the means to fund it. Neither head bothered to be innovative.[7]

From 1930, debt-funded investment was no longer an option on the table. For seventy years prior to that, famines, wars, and the Mutiny had often added to the burden of debt. But these debts were paid back from current revenues without serious problem. The large increases in military expenditure during World War I not only forced the government to borrow but since the London market was no longer easy to borrow from, the government was forced to turn towards Indian sources. During none of these episodes was Indian creditworthiness in question, because the trade was consistently in the surplus and there was enough inflow of money.

Between 1931 and 1945, the colonial system was in collapse, and a painful transition to a new order began. During the Great Depression, political unrest and weak exports reduced confidence abroad in Indian securities. The long trade boom was over. In 1931, the government could, in theory, devalue the rupee and stimulate trade. But such a step would have increased the value of India's net government remittance abroad. Fearing that India would fail to meet this commitment, London prevailed on India not to devalue but to cut expenditure instead. The massive contraction in government expenditure intensified the depression.

On budgets, the government does not stand in good light. It stands in even worse light on monetary management late in the interwar period.

The Currency Policy

The state wanted to keep trade open, which would mean that it could take no step that might reduce trade. Until World War I, trade between India and Britain was effectively free of tariffs. Free trade had adherents. But more than ideology, British manufactures needed to seek markets all over the world, and British trading firms were setting up bases in India. Indian trading firms too were not interested in anything that could regulate or reduce trade.

The primary instrument of policy in colonial India was the exchange rate. An appreciation of the rupee hurt exporters in India, and depreciation made it difficult for the budget to meet its sterling obligations. In most years, this balancing act was managed smoothly. But it became a source of controversy in the interwar period because—with debts in collapse—the objective of protecting the budgetary obligations prevailed over the objective of helping commerce.

This element of monetary dependence had always been there. To see how we need to take a close look at the exchange system. With currency reforms and unification in 1835, a modified silver standard was introduced. In other words, silver became an accepted means to settle the balance of trade. The silver rupee was further supported by a promise to mint coins on the presentation of silver bullion. There were two ways that money could be transferred between India and the rest of the world. The India Office sold Council Bills in London at an announced exchange rate, which the Exchange Banks purchased, sent to India, redeemed at the Treasury and financed trade demands for money. The receipts in London were used to meet the Home Charges. Alternatively, traders could buy silver in London, ship it to India, and have these minted into silver coins for a fee. In the last quarter of the nineteenth century, an excess supply of silver in the world led to a fall in silver prices, which made the second mode of payment the more profitable. On the recommendations of a committee of enquiry headed by Farrer Herschell, the Lord Chancellor, free coinage of silver was abolished in 1893. In 1898, on the recommendation of another committee under the direction of Henry Fowler, a Gold Exchange Standard was introduced.

The Gold Exchange Standard was in force between 1898 and 1916. The rupee was convertible against sterling and not against gold, at a ratio of 16d per rupee, or Rs. 15 for a pound sterling. To support the exchange, the India Office sold Council Bills in weekly auctions at the Bank of England. An official Gold Standard Reserve was created. It was transferred to the India Office in 1902. The reserve helped keep interests rates low in Britain. The India Office also used the Gold Standard Reserve of India in the call money market, leading to a closer alliance between the India Office and the City or the financial centre.

The Gold Exchange Standard was ordinarily trouble-free except for occasional fluctuations in the gold–silver price ratio. It was a symbol nevertheless of India's monetary dependence on Britain or the multiple heads of government that the chapter mentioned earlier. This was always potentially a controversial issue, but as long as the British and the world economy were growing no one minded. 1931 changed the mindset.

The beginning of a fall in world commodity prices in the late 1920s hurt trade. Opinion in India favoured depreciation of the rupee. But depreciation was not acceptable to London for fear that the increased burden of government remittance would lead to default. Neither of the two options usually available to the India Office in dealing with a financial crisis—fresh borrowings in London or drawing on the reserves—was practicable. The options available to the monetary authorities in India were even more limited. Devaluation was ruled out. Again, the question—what was colonial about this colonial state?—came to the fore, and now there was yet another answer available. It was colonial because London managed India's currency to serve British interest.

Eventually, on London's insistence, the government of India contracted currency, in the hope that this would reduce prices and raise demand for Indian goods. As the contraction continued, and the less it seemed to work, the harder it became to return to devaluation. For, the expected devaluation would have to be larger than before. The fall in prices raised real interest rates and rents and led to rural unrest over rent and debt. Rural assets held in the form of gold and silver began to be sold. In the next five years, these gold exports helped in the recovery. But the exports were seen as a sign of distress and left Britain–India relations impaired.

In 1935, India gained monetary autonomy with the establishment of the Reserve Bank of India. Soon enough, the Bank's activities caused a problem. The main item of currency reserve was still sterling so that any accumulation of sterling reserve led to the issue of currency. During World War II, there was a rapid accumulation of reserve because of India's contribution to the War. The result was inflation. The usual way central banks can 'sterilize' a reserve expansion is by issuing government securities. A government that would soon change hands cannot sell many securities.

Conclusion

The chapter started with a question: What was colonial about the colonial state, and was the colonial element damaging for the Indian economy? Nationalists answered the question in two ways, the state was colonial and damaging because it drained savings away; and it was colonial and damaging because London had too much control on India's monetary system. The first argument I reject because it makes little economic sense. The second argument I reject because London's interference was really damaging only in the 1930s.

I offer a third answer to the question. The colonial government was colonial by having multiple heads, one head minding the budget and another the currency. The multiple-heads damaged Indian economic interest because it forced both parties to be conservative. Simply put, British India taxed the peasants and used the money to protect trade. If it were to spend on development on a serious scale, it would need to raise more debt. This would need London and Delhi to work jointly, and against Indian opinion. Neither head risked that.

Although weak and regressive, colonial rule produced an extraordinary welfare benefit.

Notes

1. Ewout Frankema, 'Raising Revenue in the British Empire, 1870–1940: How Extractive Were Colonial Taxes?,' *Journal of Global History*, 5(3), 2010, 447–477.
2. Javier Cuenca Esteban, 'The British Balance of Payments, 1772–1820: India Transfers and War Finance,' *Economic History Review*, 54(1), 2001, 58–86.

3. Bipan Chandra, *The Rise and Growth of Economic Nationalism in India*, Delhi: People's Publishing House, 1966.
4. Dadabhai Naoroji, *Poverty and Un-British Rule in India*, London: Swan Sonnenschein, 1901, 265.
5. Patrick K. O'Brien, 'The Costs and Benefits of British Imperialism 1846–1914', *Past and Present*, 120, 1988, 163–200.
6. Tirthankar Roy, 'State Capacity and the Economic History of Colonial India,' *Australian Economic History Review*, 2018 (https://onlinelibrary.wiley.com/doi/epdf/10.1111/aehr.12166, accessed 25 October 2018).
7. A counterfactual scenario is one in which the government in India raised money domestically and made investment commitments against this capital. This would rid the system of multiple heads but would be more expensive, inflationary, and disturb trade.

References

B.R. Tomlinson, *The Political Economy of the Raj, 1914–47*, London and Basingstoke: Macmillan, 1979.

G. Balachandran, 'Colonial India and the World Economy, c. 1850–1940', in Latika Chaudhary, Bishnupriya Gupta, Tirthankar Roy, and Anand V. Swamy, eds., *A New Economic History of Colonial India*. Abingdon and London: Routledge, 2016, 84–99.

Tirthankar Roy, 'State Capacity and the Economic History of Colonial India,' *Australian Economic History Review*, 2018. https://onlinelibrary.wiley.com/doi/full/10.1111/aehr.12166 (accessed 3 February 2019).

CHAPTER 6

End of Famine

Abstract India's population began to grow rapidly from the 1920s, as death rates fell quickly, children survived early-life diseases better, and epidemics were brought under control. Innovations in medical research and communications played a significant role in ending famines. These were, partly, an indirect benefit of openness. But mortality decline was not good news for all. Mortality decline meant that more young women had to mind more children at home. Early marriage prevented many women from taking up new wage-earning opportunities. Growing family size made their economic value smaller and lives at home harder than before.

Keywords Population growth · Women in India · Famine · Epidemics in India · Public health

The history of welfare in colonial India was one of much bad news and one big good news. India's population, long stagnant or growing slowly, began to grow rapidly from the 1920s thanks to a permanent fall in mortality. What had changed? Why did people live longer? Was it good news for everyone?

The chapter shows that innovations in medical research and communications played a significant role in ending famines. These innovations did not follow a well-designed policy to end famines. Rather, they were the unintended consequences of openness. India was not an attractive

© The Author(s) 2019
T. Roy, *How British Rule Changed India's Economy*,
Palgrave Studies in Economic History,
https://doi.org/10.1007/978-3-030-17708-9_6

destination for British wage-earners. But it was a lucrative field of employment for skilled European workers hired by factories, hospitals, newspapers, schools, colleges, laboratories, railways, telegraph, ports, ships, and offices. These people helped build and run the railways and helped research on epidemics, and in this way, openness aided the fall in mortality.

Here is a paradox—the mortality decline changed Indian society in an adverse way. Women were married early in India. A mortality decline meant that more young women had to mind more children at home. Early marriage prevented many women from taking up the new wage-earning opportunities that appeared in towns and cities far away from home. Growing family size made their economic value smaller and lives at home harder than before.

First, the good news.

Population Growth

Population growth is shaped by three things: the economic rationality of having large or small families, cultural preference for large or small families, and health care systems and nutritional status, which shape human ability to control or cope with biological processes. The different speeds with which these factors change lead to periods of high or low population growth.

The demographic transition theory plots the changing relationship between these variables on a time scale. In premodern times, death rates were high owing to diseases and famines. It would make sense to produce many children. Religion, moral codes, and custom approved of early marriage, universal marriage, and high fertility. Net population growth would be small. From the nineteenth century, death rates started to fall because of improved health care and nutrition. But birth rates stayed high because customs persisted. The world saw higher population growth. Eventually, families saw the economic costs of having large families to be excessive and customs weakened. More women working for wages meant more women regarding the time spent on children as lost wages. Costlier education meant more parents minded the cost of raising children. Societies experienced a fall in fertility and in the rate of population growth. In most developing countries, this demographic transition started later than in Europe but was speedier. The decline of mortality was relatively quick thanks to basic technologies for disease and epidemic control. But fertility stayed high because in agricultural societies labour was highly valued.

The mortality transition happened in India around 1920. Systematic census began from 1881. Many years before then, officers of the East India Company had realized the administrative need for population data but did not always have the means to carry out large-scale surveys. For the pre-1881 period, and especially for the pre-British period, various people measured population growth using different assumptions. One study, using a somewhat acceptable method, suggests that population growth in 1801–1871 was close to zero.[1] In the first half of the census period (1872–1921), the population growth rate was again close to zero, because of famines in 1876, 1896, and 1899, and the influenza epidemic of 1918–1919. But thereafter, the growth rate increased because the mortality rate declined quickly from 1921, whereas fertility rate did not change much. From 42–50 per thousand in the decade 1911–1921, the death rate fell to 33–38 in the next decade, 30–32 in 1931–1941 and 25 in 1941–1951. The birth rate fell marginally, from 45–49 per thousand persons in 1911–1921 to 40–42 in 1941–1951. Consequently, the population began to grow much faster from 1921.

In world history, there are two explanations for mortality decline. One of these stresses public health measures that led to better treatment of communicable diseases, such as malaria eradication, immunization, improved sanitation, and antibiotics. A second view says that these measures were not popular before mortality began to decline, and therefore, improvement in nutrition and better resistance to diseases were the real reason. Disease treatment and nutritional improvement did have an effect in India. For example, child mortality rate fell from 200 in 1901 to 180 in 1931 to 116 in 1951. This level did not compare too badly with the poorer countries in South America or even Europe, though it was still among the world's highest.

Public health and nutrition do not completely explain India's transition, because famines were the main cause of mass death in India before 1900 and the disappearance of famines after 1900 the main reason for the fall in death rate. This did not happen due to medical intervention alone, nor better nutrition for all, but a better distribution of food between shortage areas and surplus areas. As the railways grew in density and reach, and long-distance trade in foodgrain expanded, grain could move into scarcity areas much faster than before in response to higher prices of grain.

So, both public health and the railways were important. Let me first discuss medical intervention.

Public Health

Treatment of common tropical diseases using local knowledge and local material was a life and death issue for European surgeons who came to India in the seventeenth and eighteenth century. Common diseases killed Europeans readily and the remedies were unknown to them. They understood that the medical profession in India was well-developed, used written manuals and codes, and were headed by an educated elite. In principle, it should be easy to translate and codify such knowledge. Despite a few successful projects (such as the *Hortus Malabaricus*, 1678–1693, prepared under the direction of Hendrik van Rheede, the Dutch governor in Kerala), collaboration with the Indian doctors did not happen on a large enough scale and there was nothing like a fusion of the two systems.

In the early nineteenth century, western medicine and doctors kept an open mind about local remedies for common diseases. The situation changed in the late nineteenth century, when development in western medicine and surgery, new notions of hygiene and the germ theory of disease, created a wide gulf between indigenous and western systems in their conceptual tools. This separation was deep only in the institutions of teaching and learning. Individual doctors often kept an open mind. Still, the hierarchy may have led to some loss of indigenous knowledge.

In the end, doctors and treatment had a lesser role in the mortality decline than the discovery of the cause of the disease and the public health measures that followed. In this enterprise, the colonial medical service scored significant breakthroughs. A government medical service started in 1785 mainly to serve the needs of the army. It was open to the public but had limited capacity to serve the public. In 1896, the many heads were joined to form the Indian Medical Service.

The Service was always short of people, money for research, and outreach. Its poor capacity to deal with epidemics and famines was exposed time and again. But it did not stop its employees from doing research on their own time and using government laboratories for the purpose. This freedom was used much in the same way in which Company doctors had researched Indian diseases in earlier times. It was experimental and exploratory in nature. But around 1900, thanks to better scientific knowledge and better instruments, the research began to produce some remarkable successes.

Ronald Ross' work on the malaria parasite (1897) was an example. Between 1882 and 1927, 'fever', the generic term for malaria, accounted for about two-thirds of all deaths. Malaria had a close association with agricultural expansion because new cultivation zones often had pools of dammed up water. As a better understanding of causation emerged, the frequency of deaths from the disease fell.

Cholera was common in the army barracks, religious fairs, market-places, and towns. Until the 1870s, doctors and sanitary commissioners disagreed on whether the disease was airborne or waterborne. By the 1890s, there was agreement on the causes, and cholera mortality started to fall rapidly thereafter. The first breakthrough with leprosy was achieved in the 1880s with the finding that the disease spread through contact, which led to the creation of leprosy asylums. By 1910, knowledge on the disease had improved and shown that bad nutrition and sanitation had more to do with its spread than casual contact. The number that suffered started to fall rapidly thereafter.

From its first major appearance in Bombay in 1896–1938, when plague almost disappeared, the disease claimed twelve million lives. The plague bacilli were native to the Himalayan foothills and the Western Ghats in Mysore. But a combination of circumstances made it travel fast in these years. These were crowding and malnutrition. Both cholera and malaria had an association with famines and scarcity, but the plague did not. All three hurt the poor more than the rich. Plague also affected certain professions, for example, grain dealers, who were more exposed to infected rats.

The cities enabled public health officers to observe how epidemics touched some settlements and spared others, even when these were located side by side. That knowledge of the distribution of epidemics was crucial to understanding the role of sanitation practices. For example, in the 1890s, the Plague Research Committee made the important discovery that the plague bacillus spread through human excrement, again showing how poor sanitation in the city slums made some of these diseases impossible to control.

Not just doctors and public health professionals, intellectuals in the big city too noticed that epidemics discriminated between the middle class and the slum dwellers and publicized the discovery in their own fashion. They did not just publish pamphlets, but wrote poetry. B. F. Patell, a teacher in the Elphinstone School, an eye-witness, and a poet of the plague, wrote:

> The European race I mean, untouched who 'scaped Plague's horrors clean.
> Themselves secure, their courage rose while witnessing their neighbours' woes;
> Right in the city they remained, a fearless attitude maintained;
> See, open all their business places; their games and sports and annual races.

The city administration segregated the slum dwellers as if to shelter the sports-loving Europeans. But this was a pointless and unpopular step. Things needed to change within the slums. Eventually, the sanitary staff tracked individuals to identify the trail of the disease and cut off infection. Fewer people thereafter shared Patell's lament that 'science avails not, so cruel the Fates!'[2]

Smallpox was a worldwide killer in the eighteenth and nineteenth century, and India was no exception. Although the smallpox vaccine was discovered in 1796, throughout the nineteenth century, its diffusion was slow. Hospital records show that in 1852, the smallpox fatality rate (deaths per affected population) was as high as 42% in Calcutta. Fatality rates, however, dropped to less than 25 in rural areas. Smallpox mortality fell mainly due to the end of famines.

While medical intervention brought down mortality among all sections of the population exposed to the common pathogen, the end of famine brought down mortality among the rural poor of vulnerable regions. Why did famines disappear? To answer the question, we need to know why they happened in the first place.

End of Famines

Famines, defined as episodes of acute starvation on a large scale, were a frequent occurrence in India until 1900. However, it is impossible to construct any sensible history of the frequency or intensity of famines in the long run. We cannot be sure if famines were more frequent or less frequent during British rule compared with past rules. The required sources do not exist for periods before the early-1800s. From 1770, famines were discussed by government officers. The 1880 Famine Commission recommended the foundation of a Department of Agriculture, which would collect data on weather and crops, and warn farmers of bad seasons ahead. The Census and registers of vital statistics collected data every year on births and deaths, which showed better why and when famines began. By contrast, the pre-1770 data came from biographies of rulers, chronicles of military exploits, and travelogues. These are not reliable sources of historical statistics.

Mixing sources can lead to misleading conclusions about the long history of famines. Historians of Indian famines have often fallen in that trap. For example, one of the best-known works on Indian famines, *Famines in India* by B. M. Bhatia, estimates that 'in the earlier times a major famine occurred once every 50 years', whereas 'between 1860 and 1908, famine or scarcity prevailed in .. twenty out of the total of forty-nine years'.[3] His source was Alexander Loveday, a Cambridge scholar who wrote an essay on Indian famines in 1914.[4] Loveday did not do any original research but prepared an appendix listing known famines since the beginning of the Common Era. Whereas the post-1800 famines were recorded by the government statistical system, the pre-1800 data came from hagiographies and travelogues. The frequency with which famines occurred in these earlier times depended on the frequency with which hagiographies were written. If this was once in fifty years, we would conclude that famines happened once in fifty years, as Bhatia did. It makes no sense.

Official record on famines started from 1769–1770. The 1769–1770 famine in Bengal followed two years of erratic rainfall worsened by a smallpox epidemic. An 1812–1813 famine in western India, which affected the Kathiawar region especially, came in the wake of several years of crop loss due to attacks by locusts and rats. The legendary Guntur famine of 1832–1833 followed crop failure as well as excessive and uncertain levels of taxation on peasants. In at least three episodes in nineteenth-century western India—1819–1820 in Broach, 1820–1822 in Sind, and 1853 in Thana and Colaba—famines were caused by monsoon flooding. The 1865–1867 famine in coastal Orissa followed several seasons of erratic rainfall but was worsened by the refusal of the local administration to import food.

In the last quarter of the nineteenth century, major famines causing in excess of a million deaths occurred thrice, 1876–1878, 1896–1897, and 1899–1900. In each case, there were successive crop failures of unusual intensity in the Deccan plateau. In the twentieth century, major famines were fewer. In 1907–1908, an extensive crop failure and epidemic threat was effectively tackled by state relief machinery. Food procurement for World War II, combined with crop failure, caused the harshest famine of the twentieth century, the 1943 Bengal famine. This was an unusual event on many levels and cannot be compared with the other famines cited before. I return to this episode later.

Famines happened because of a sharp, sudden, and sustained rise in food prices. While it affected all poor people, the effect could be direct or indirect. For example, when food prices rose, people purchased less cloth, which meant that artisans had less money to buy food. Peasants usually had some storage of grain. The agricultural labourers, like the artisans, did not. The 1876 famine drove large numbers of rural labourers and handloom weavers of South India to enlist for emigration to British tropical colonies abroad. The 1896 and 1899 famines again encouraged migration (Fig. 6.1). Famines also affected land transfers between the poor and the richer peasants, but these effects are not well-researched.

Fig. 6.1 Famine 1900. One of the last great famines, the 1899–1900 famine recorded a high death rate from diseases (© Photo 12/Alamy Stock Photo)

Almost every known famine in India before 1900 started because of failure of rains, usually failure for two successive seasons. In 1876–1878 and 1896–1898 Madras and Bombay famines, the first few months after a harvest failure saw a rise in food prices, and rise in deaths. Deaths were more common among men, who left home in search of work, among the children and the elderly, and among the lower castes, engaged in labour and craft work. Crop failure drove people to change diets and forage in the forests and commons. In the first few months of starvation, fodder and seeds were eaten up, so that cattle died in large numbers. This would make a return to cultivation difficult after the next normal rains. Towards the end of a famine, malnutrition reduced biological resistance to smallpox, plague, cholera, pneumonia, diarrhoea, and malaria.

Crop failure was only the immediate trigger. Why did crop failure cause mass deaths? Why did *famines* occur? We should expect from a good theory of famines the ability to explain both what factors caused them in the first place, and why they disappeared eventually (the same causal forces should have become weaker than before). Most theories of Indian famines fail the test.

In the early nineteenth century, there was a view that overpopulation caused famines. The priest-cum-economist Thomas Malthus had said (around 1800) that too many people trying to compete for limited food would lead to famines. Malthus' influence upon officers in India was large. His theory had the message that the state should not interfere when a famine happened.[5] The nineteenth-century famines did not support his theory. The Deccan famines happened in areas of low population density, whereas the most densely populated Indo-Gangetic Basin largely escaped famines after 1783. Government enquiries after these episodes, therefore, did not follow Malthus.

The Reports of the Indian Famine Commission (1880, 1898, 1901, and the Famine Enquiry Commission Report of 1945), the Report of the Indian Irrigation Commission (1901–1908), and Famine Codes (1880, and provincial codes to follow) said that famines happened because of a risky agrarian environment. In a tropical region, water was a scarcer resource than land. When monsoon rain was the main source of water, a big risk attached to the supply of water. Not all regions were equally affected, of course. But those 'poor in soil, their rain-fall precarious, little .. artificial irrigation [were] severely affected whenever drought visited'.[6]

This is the ecological account of famines. The ecological theory said that the state had a role to play in prevention and cure. It led to the formation of an emergency-response or a relief system, and justification for government investment in irrigation canals. In the late-1800s, administrators advocated irrigation works and restoration of disused tanks as insurance against future famines. A clear policy on relief did not take shape until 1880. There was resistance within the administration to expenditure on irrigation, which, it was felt, brought uncertain returns. A state agency in relief, it was said, interfered with the working of the market. The ferocity of the 1876 famine reduced these resistances.

The ecological theory, thus, delivered a good outcome. But it cannot explain why famines disappeared after 1900. Surely, the geographical condition did not change? Something else changed to mitigate the worst effects of natural disasters. What was that something?

Among Indian nationalists, the prevailing view was that globalization caused famines. Shortly after the famine of 1896–1898, some Indian bureaucrats and nationalist writers, such as K. L. Datta and R. C. Dutt, suggested that the export of foodgrains from India had reduced domestic food availability during periods of bad harvest, and thus increased the intensity of famines. Questioning this view, sections of the bureaucracy held that foreign trade stabilized consumption, for exports increased when domestic prices were low and good harvests had created a surplus over consumption needs, while exports fell when prices were high. In hindsight, Datta et al. were wrong on another point too: famines ended by 1900 even though free trade did not. An almost identical twin to this theory claimed that colonial indifference caused mass deaths during famines. Again, this cannot be right because famines ended when colonialism still ruled.

The debate raises the question: Did trade mitigate famines or caused them? Michelle McAlpin examined this topic for the Bombay Presidency, showing that markets and railways in fact improved food distribution enough to reduce the impact of harvest failure. In several regions (called vanguards in Chapter 4), canal irrigation reduced the chances of severe crop failure, and thus reduced the impact of famines. These effects followed not only from local increases in production but also from the easier movement of crops, which the railways had made possible. Trade was also an incentive to grow more food.

Recent research on food markets (see Chapter 1 for citation) and on famines support McAlpin's thesis that the railways led to a better and faster distribution of food, and a reduction in the impact of famines. Similarly, information about local agricultural conditions was limited and travelled slowly, which affected the quality and speed of response to famines in the nineteenth century.[7] Such information improved in quality and quantity. Christopher Bayly and more recently Steven G. Marks suggest that European rule and modern capitalism were heavy users of information. The weather office and the agricultural office in colonial India would support that.[8]

None of these theories discuss famine relief organized by the government. In precolonial India, the prospect of famines had encouraged the construction of state granaries which were used for relief purposes. Common measures to prevent famines were tanks and canals. Private and temple charity was also at work. But both the granaries and the private systems were local and too small in scale to matter much. In the early nineteenth century, the Company left famine relief to the local princes. In the mid-nineteenth century, local administration was more deeply engaged than before, but no clear coordinated policy was in place.

The ecological theory of famines changed that. Between 1876 and 1896, a systematic relief infrastructure was set up in British India. The main element of the policy was relief camps where starving persons could receive food in exchange of labour at public works projects, such as the construction of railways or irrigation canals. A Famine Insurance Fund was started in 1881, out of which relief-related expenditures were to be funded.

The relief camp idea was not unknown in 1876 or before, but its scale was limited, the labour requirement was rarely enforced due to a shortage of supervisors, and entry was based on the degree of distress, which was hard to define and subject to abuse. By the end of the century, the relief camp worked better in Madras and Bombay Presidencies and could mobilize thousands of labourers for construction works. It had many problems. Many seekers of relief, such as the artisans, could not offer the kind of labour the camps wanted and paid for. Some did not want to eat the same food as others did due to caste prejudices. Women often avoided the camps. The Famine Codes became lengthier to accommodate such complexity.

Now, the bad news. While the mortality rate fell, birth rate did not change. Why not, and what was the consequence?

High Birth Rate and the Status of Women in India

In theory, the smaller the chance of survival of children the more would parents want large families. This simple reason may explain why birth rates in India were high and high enough to match the death rate. There were social measures to ensure a high birth rate. The most effective measure was to get women married early.

The mean age at marriage in India was one of the lowest in the world and rose slowly in the twentieth century. The mean age at marriage for women in India was 13 in the decade 1891–1901, and 16 in the decade 1951–1961. The age was lowest by far by any contemporary standard. In 1920, the mean age for women in Japan was 23. In Europe, the age was 25 or more even at the beginning of industrialization. In neighbouring Burma and Ceylon, the average age for women in the first decade of the twentieth century was 18–20.

With the average age as low as this, few girls had the chance to work and earn money before they were married and had children to look after. The participation of women in commercial work for wages was also one of the lowest in India. Most women worked from home. Since education was of little value to them, they were not educated. The level of female literacy was zero before 1901. Nor did many women have property of their own. The marriage custom involved a social attitude that did not see women as productive workers, and therefore, did not see them as legitimate claimants to property. High infant mortality reflected the poor health of the mothers, in turn, a result of child marriage, frequency of motherhood, primitive obstetrics, and unsanitary conditions.

Social customs that suppressed women could, paradoxically, reduce birth rates too, if only locally. There were about 1030–1070 males per 1000 females in 1881–1931. In north India, there was an excess of males, and in south India, there was an excess of females. Three hypotheses have been offered to explain the excess of males in the north, under-enumeration of females, under-reporting of female births, and greater risks of death for women both at birth and at the time of child-bearing. The third kind of risk arose from social biases against the girl child. They arose more specifically from such practices as female infanticide among some communities, and the neglect of female infants and children. A high female-to-male ratio did not necessarily mean a good deal for the females. It could mean instead that there was a lot of emigration, for migration was male-biased to an unusual extent in India.

Women's health was a disgrace, a scandal, of colonial India. The bad situation had owed to the way the parents treated their daughters. It was a cultural problem. 'The laws of society', wrote Norman Chevers, a medical officer and author of a book on medical jurisprudence (1886), 'exercise the most rigorous and vigilant control imaginable over the conduct of females'. In rural Bengal, girls married early, were often widowed in their twenties. More than eighty per cent of the widows did not marry again, had limited right of property, and relied on the dubious support of their relatives. The police routinely investigated cases of abortion by methods that killed the mother, and murders of infants. Local experts told the judges that only a fraction of the cases where a serious injury was involved in trying to hide or end pregnancy actually led to police action. Although child marriage was common, Hindu and Muslim codes frowned upon cohabitation before puberty. A few police cases, however, were reported where a prepubescent girl died as a result of what would now be described as child abuse and marital rape combined. Anything less than death went unreported.

Rising births and early marriage robbed millions of girls of their childhood. They were workers first and foremost, surrogate mothers, until the time they became mothers themselves. In 1896, a young zamindar observed a girl of about eight or nine, member of a migrant working family, and wrote a poem in her honour,[9]

> They dig by the river for bricklaying - labourers from the west country. Their little girl
> keeps scampering to the ghat. Such scrubbing and scouring
> of pots and pans and dishes! Comes running
> a hundred times a day, brass bangles jangling
> clang clang against the brass plates she cleans.
>
> So busy all day! Her little brother,
> bald, mud-daubed, not a stitch on his limbs,
> follows her like a pet, patiently sits
> on the high bank, as Big Sister commands.
> Plates against her left side, a full pitcher on her head,
> the girl goes back, the child's hand in her right hand.
> A surrogate of her mother,
> bent under her work-load, such a wee Big Sister!

We will make a mistake to think that this is a poem about poverty, class, or migrant labour. It is a poem about lost girlhood. Little girls even in richer and middle-class families for generations to come worked as the surrogate mother for a growing number of siblings.

India practiced child marriage, but there were regional variations. The age at marriage was the lowest in eastern India (Greater Bengal, eastern UP, but not Assam), and parts of central India. Age of consent law existed in British India but was universally disregarded until the enactment of the Child Marriage Restraint Act of 1930. This act made the marriage of women below the age of 14 punishable, if not invalid. The Act was no more than a piece of paper for a long time after it was passed. Marriages were held in public places in open defiance. Different religious communities had different views on it. In western India, marriages could be held a few miles away from the village, inside the territory of a native state where British laws did not apply. Nevertheless, the Act and the few actual convictions under it had a mild deterrent effect after 1930.

As the average age at marriage started to creep up, the effect of bad tradition became weaker. To my knowledge, no good study is available on why the average age at marriage increased in twentieth-century India. One would assume that education, social reform movements, and medical care that aided fall in death rates, all had a role to play. The cities, especially the cosmopolitan port cities, were far more progressive on women's education, marriage customs, and women's role in public affairs. The one factor that did not have much of a role was employment prospect, which worsened rather than improved for women.

Between 1881 (colonial India) and 1951 (Indian Union), work-participation rate fell from 43% of the population to 39. These participation rates capture participation in commercial work, that is, work that carried a payment or a monetary return. The fall is normal if the proportion of younger people increases, or if more children join the school and work less for money. In these years, the age-composition of the population remained roughly stable. School enrolment and literacy did increase slowly, and this factor did reduce participation rates. But a significant difference remained between men and women.

The male participation rate fell from 63 to 54%, and women's participation fell from 31 to 23%. Fewer women went to school whether at the beginning of the period or at the end. The participation rate was low because most women worked inside homes. The proportion of those women who did work outside fell relatively more than the proportion for men. Compared with the men, women *retreated* from commercial work, not because more went to school but more stayed at home.

Men and women in all societies face differential chances of a move into the wage labour market. The difference arises because of the need, in the case of women, to accommodate wage-work into the domestic routine, in which the care of small children is the most crucial task. Before modern industrialization began, women in artisanal families did industrial work, the family home itself was the place of work, and the balancing of domestic with commercial work did not pose a problem. But it did become a problem as work began to shift outside the home. To continue working, women needed to leave home and children for some time during the day, which was not easy.

In many past societies, this difficulty shows up in the shape of two tendencies. First, women's participation in urban industrial labour fell for many years, and then, as childcare and home duties became easier to manage, started rising. In the course of industrialization, the percentage of women in the urban industrial labour market followed a U-shape. Secondly, age-wise women's participation rate peaked for a group in which adult unmarried girls formed a majority, for example, 15–24 years, the rate then fell in a group in which the majority were married with small children, and the rate rose again when many among the married women returned to work. If the over-time rate follows a U-shape, the across-age rate follows an M-shape.

In India, marriage customs modified the expected patterns. The low age at marriage meant that few young adults joined the workforce (or the absence of an M-shape), and consequently, most potential workers found it difficult to leave home and enter the factory as work shifted from home to factory (a long decline phase in the U-curve, see Figs. 6.2 and 6.3). We find both these predictions to be correct from census data. Even those women who offered their services faced a variety of obstacles in joining the city labour markets, including legislation that made employers less willing to hire women. And, therefore, the high birth rate continued (Fig. 6.4).

So far I have shown why mortality rates fell, birth rates did not, and why the combination was a mixed blessing for society. Throughout, I have made scant reference to the last of the major famines in British India, the Great Bengal Famine of 1943. This oversight now needs

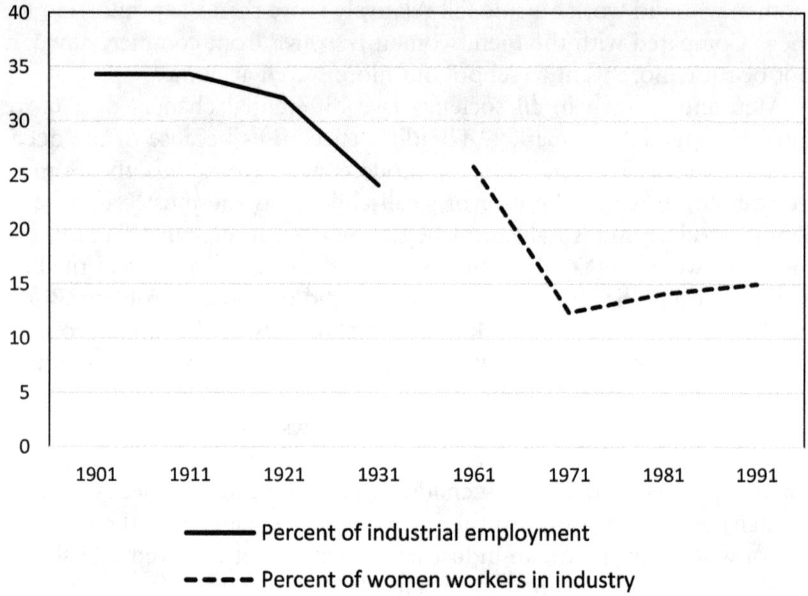

Fig. 6.2 Women workers in industry 1901–1991 (Undivided India till 1961, Indian Union after 1961)

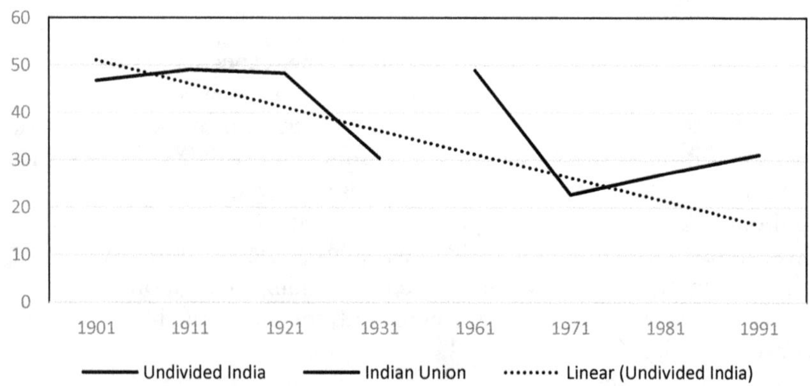

Fig. 6.3 The ratio of women-men work-participation rate (%)

correction. In recent years, debates around this one episode have driven the whole discourse on why famines occurred. I have claimed earlier that the example does not overturn or affect any of the conclusions that we

Fig. 6.4 Mother India (1957). Mother India was a retort to Katherine Mayo's infamous book of the same name published thirty years before (Chapter 1). The film celebrated the courage of a woman and her family against adversities and the harassments of an evil moneylender. At the time this proud patriotic statement about Indian womanhood appeared, Indian womanhood was doing badly, married in their teens, shut out from paid work by migrant men, and minding more children than a generation before (© TCD/Prod.DB/Alamy Stock Photo)

can draw on the link between famine and population trends (see also Fig. 1.2, Chapter 1). A question still remains to be answered.

Does the Bengal Famine have *any lesson at all*?

The Bengal Famine

Before the Partition of India, the British Indian province Bengal included the territory of Bangladesh and the West Bengal state in India. The 1943 famine happened in this province because the price of rice, the main staple, rose more than three times between February and September. With the Japanese occupation of Burma in 1942, the border between Bengal and Burma became the eastern front of World War II. Requisition of rice to feed the soldiers stationed here increased the demand for rice (Fig. 6.5). But Bengal was an agriculturally developed region, had good transportation, and a stable government. A fresh supply of rice should be easy to arrange. Why did supplies fail?

Fig. 6.5 Men of the Royal Air Force feeding local children, 1943. The job of feeding soldiers aggravated the 1943 famine in Bengal. Soldiers, however, took an active part in famine relief (© Trinity Mirror/Mirrorpix/Alamy Stock Photo)

Numerous scholars have searched for an answer to the question.[10] One reason for an overload of scholarship on the subject is that the economist Amartya Sen offered a controversial argument on why the famine happened. Famines, he said, can occur not because of a harvest shortfall caused by bad weather, but due to human agency. In the case of the Bengal Famine, the human agency was triggered by the World War. Food was hoarded. Sen's argument that the famine happened without a bad harvest disputed the explanation offered by the Famine Inquiry Commission, which had said there was a shortage. Many others felt compelled to test Sen's claim, revise it, or challenge it.

The evidence on this episode, however, does not support any claim conclusively. Sen's claim is difficult to test, because of the way crop statistics were collected in British India. Between one year and the next, the statistical office would measure changes in cropped areas and then apply a standard or average productivity in order to estimate the total output. In other words, the system was able to record change if low prices in one year led farmers to sow a smaller area. But it was not good at recording change if there was, say, flood damage or disease. An astute officer could revise the yield figure downward but to do so unilaterally was unusual. This problem has led several scholars to revise the crop output data, including Mark Tauger, Peter Bowbrick, Omkar Goswami and Mufakharul Islam. Their work shows that the harvest size *probably fell.*

The global history of famines shows that sometimes when the administration is a dictatorship, a single political party or a warlord, and directly controlled food distribution, culpability for a famine can be fixed without question. Alex De Waal, a researcher of African famines, has described such famines as holocausts, genocides or atrocities. Some contributors to the debate suggest in this spirit that the despotic British imperialists deliberately starved the Bengalis. This is simplistic. Bengal did not have a despotic rule in this time. Although India was still ruled by the British, provinces were ruled by elected governments. The administration was a government formed by a democratic process. Food was distributed by the free market and was not subject to command and control. The little command and control the government did try to impose were not very effective because the government had few resources.

Democracy as Bengal had did not help. Within the government, between ministers, and between the ministers and bureaucrats, there was fierce conflict, rivalry, and misinformation about the famine. The most powerful opinion was that there was no shortage of food in Bengal and that grain traders were secretly stocking up on food in order to cause an artificial shortage. In 1943, the key decision-maker in the government was the Minister of Civil Supplies, Hussein Suhrawardy. Throughout the famine, he was an aggressive campaigner for the no-shortage theory, and throughout, his colleagues, critics, and officers contradicted him. This quarrelsome bunch of relief-givers weakened and delayed response.

Madhusree Mukherjee in her book, *Churchill's Secret War* (2010) lays the blame at the door of London. She says that Winston Churchill, the British prime minister, held racist views about Indians which prevented Britain from supplying enough relief to Bengal in time. As political history, the argument is naïve. There is little evidence that Churchill's personal views about Indians influenced the policies of the War Cabinet. With Japan's entry into the war and the fall of Singapore in February 1942, the British Empire's resources were a critical asset for Britain to fight a war that stretched from Europe to North Africa to Asia. A potential obstacle to using this resource was the local nationalist movement. Churchill's reactionary views on the empire notwithstanding, the context for almost everything he said about Indians and the empire was related to the Indian nationalist movement. Negotiating with the Indian nationalists during the War could be pointless and dangerous because the moderate nationalists were demoralized by dissensions and the radical nationalists wanted the axis powers to win on the eastern front. Racist or not, no Prime Minister would be willing to fight a war and negotiate with the nationalists at the same time.

What has any of that to do with the famine? Very little. The War Cabinet did not divert enough ships from the theatres of war to Bengal or order India to divert army rations to feeding people because the Cabinet believed what the Bengalis told it: there was no shortage of food in Bengal. The Cabinet took decisions in the knowledge that the axis powers were sinking one ship every day and had sunk around a million tons of shipping in 1942. The regions where rice might be available were the most dangerous waters to enter. Army rations were already reduced. Further cuts could risk a mutiny.

Administration, London, the Famine Inquiry Commission—and Amartya Sen—believed that grain merchants were hoarding food. It is not surprising that merchants were blamed during famines. Merchants were blamed for every famine that occurred in India during the nineteenth century. Most of the time, the charge was overstated. It was extremely dangerous for a grain merchant to stockpile food during a famine. They could get killed in a food riot and, on occasion, they were killed. The administration acted on the belief and started raiding merchant warehouses. The merchants were Hindus, so the Hindu political outfit, the Hindu Mahasabha, protested, while the Communists insisted the merchants were to blame. What did the administration find? Some excess stocks of kerosene, sugar, coal. But few traders were found with and prosecuted for excess stock of rice. Given the immense scale of the shortage, hoarding was inconsequential.

The Bengal Famine of 1943 has never been explained. It offers no definite lesson. The culpability of either Nature, or Administration, or London, or Market has not been proven. In any case, and without meaning to make light of the enormous human tragedy of 1943, the so-called Great Bengal Famine was not really that great a disruption to the trend in life expectancy in India, which had turned upward decades ago.

Conclusion

Indians lived longer from 1920, thanks to better epidemic control, better theories of disease causation and treatment, and the disappearance of famines after 1900. The end of famine came because of better distribution of foodgrains, improvements in knowledge and information about agricultural conditions, and famine relief. Some of those same factors that had produced business growth by making science and technology accessible to Indians also produced the mortality decline.

Almost everywhere else in the population story, bad custom prevailed. Birth rates, adverse sex ratio of women, women's health, women's status in society, and the low value they commanded as commercial workers, changed little. Some of these features were reinforced. Even as commercialization encouraged work participation and occupational mobility for men, it discouraged participation and occupational mobility among women. Better value for men came with a devaluation of women. Could the state do more to change these conditions? Possibly, but not without a strong public demand for a change. There was no such demand in Indian society. Indians accepted the poor deal that women got in colonial India, and the British got away by doing little to change it.

So far I have discussed the economic history of India under colonial rule. The colonial rule came in two forms, direct rule over British India, and indirect rule over the princely states. Princely states were independent rulers. Did their independence make for a different experience?

Notes

1. P.C. Mahalanobis and D. Bhattacharya, 'Growth of Population in India and Pakistan, 1801–1961,' *Artha Vijnana*, 18(1), 1976, 1–10.
2. B.F. Patell, *History of the Plague in Bombay*, Bombay: Caxton Works, n.d.
3. B.M. Bhatia, *Famines in India*, Third Edition, Delhi: Konark, 1991, 7.
4. Alexander Loveday, *The History and Economics of Indian Famines*, London: G. Bell, 1914.
5. S. Ambirajan, 'Malthusian Population Theory and Indian Famine Policy in the Nineteenth Century,' *Population Studies*, 30(1), 1976, 5–14.
6. India, *Report of the Indian Famine Commission. Part I: Famine Relief*, London: HMSO, 1880, 5.
7. Tirthankar Roy, *Natural Disasters and Indian History*, New Delhi: Oxford University Press, 2012.
8. Christopher Bayly, *Empire and Information: Intelligence Gathering and Social Communication in India, 1780–1870*, Cambridge: Cambridge University Press, 1996; Steven G. Marks, *The Information Nexus: Global Capitalism from the Renaissance to the Present*, Cambridge: Cambridge University Press, 2016.
9. Rabindranath Tagore, Big Sister, translated by Ketaki Kushari Dyson (*I Won't Let You Go*, Highgreen: Bloodaxe Books, 2010, 115).
10. Contemporaries like Tarakchandra Das, Manilal Nanavati, and P.C. Mahalanobis, and later scholars like Amartya Sen, Mark Tauger, Peter Bowbrick, Cormac Ó Gráda, Mufakharul Islam, Lance Brennan, Madhusree Mukherjee, Sugata Bose, Richard Stevenson, Omkar Goswami, Auriol Law-Smith, Deepak R. Basu, Janam Mukherjee, and Paul Greenough. If we include those who studied the famine in relation to Bengal history, communalism, demography or the Second World War, then the list also contains Partha Chatterjee, Claude Markovits, Iftekhar Iqbal, Indivar Kamtekar, Kaushik Roy, Tim Dyson, Arup Maharatna, Rakesh Batabyal, and Utsa Patnaik.

Further Reading

A.K. Sen, *Poverty and Famines: An Essay on Entitlement and Deprivation*, Oxford: Oxford University Press, 1983.

Cormac Ó Gráda, 'Revisiting the Bengal Famine of 1943–4,' *History Ireland*, 18(4), 2010, 36–39.

M.B. McAlpin, *Subject to Famine: Food Crisis and Economic Change in Western India, 1860–1920*, Princeton: Princeton University Press, 1983.

M.U. Mushtaq, 'Public Health in British India: A Brief Account of the History of Medical Services and Disease Prevention in Colonial India,' *Indian Journal of Community Medicine*, 34(1), 2009, 6–14.

Tim Dyson, *Population History of India*, Oxford: Clarendon Press, 2018.

CHAPTER 7

A Different Story? The Princely States

Abstract The princely states were the kingdoms that British India did not annex to itself. The states lived under an agreement with British India, the two main points of the agreement were that they would keep trade open and would not raise an army. How were the states affected by colonialism? Does their history change the main story of this book? This chapter shows that it does not.

Keywords Princely states · Imperialism · Indirect rule · Regional inequality in India · Railways

The princely states were the kingdoms that British India did not annex to itself. The states were allies of the British, and those in northern India had demonstrated the loyalty during the great mutiny (1857). After this event, the Crown took over power in India and announced a stop to further conquest. Thereafter, the states lived under an agreement with British India, the two main points of the agreement were that they would keep trade open and would not raise an army. A British resident stationed in or near the capital city of a state observed the regime, and in some cases (like Mysore), took a big part in running it. The states ruled over 40–45% of the area of India and 25% of the population (Map 7.1).

© The Author(s) 2019

T. Roy, *How British Rule Changed India's Economy*,
Palgrave Studies in Economic History,
https://doi.org/10.1007/978-3-030-17708-9_7

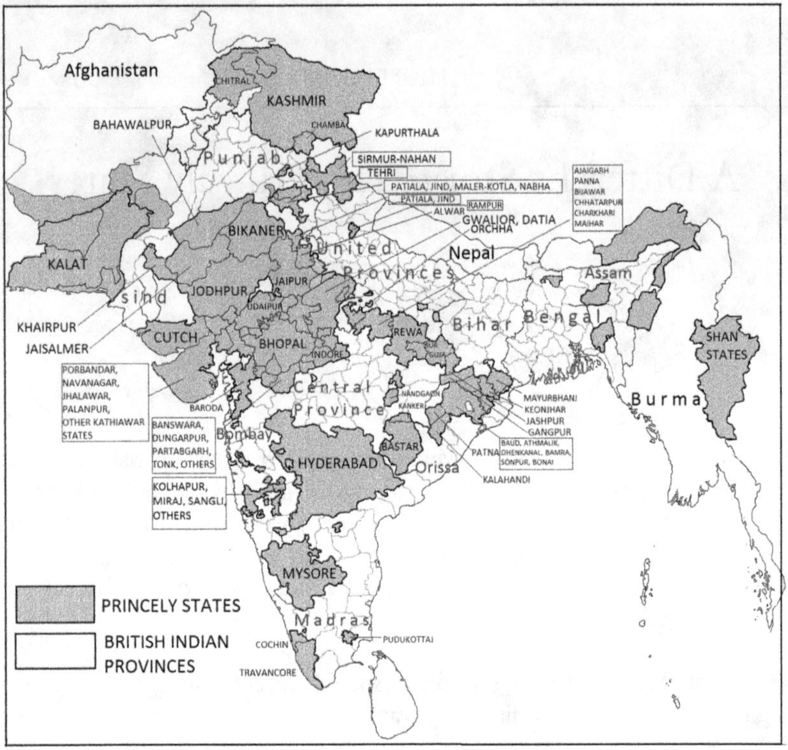

Map 7.1 Major princely states

How were the states affected by colonialism? Does their history change the main story of this book? I show in this chapter that it does not.

We should be interested in these questions for a reason. If the colonial policy was bad economics, surely independence would be good for economic development? I show here that the states and British India were more similar than different. Why did independence not deliver a lot more development in the states? There are two possible answers. Either independence did not necessarily mean greater willingness to foster development. Think of the princes lavishly spending money on jewellery, horses, and mistresses. Or the princely states were limited in their capacity to foster development. This second hypothesis is in spirit closer to the one that Chapter 5 established, that the colonial state had limited capacity. The chapter sides with the second view.

Much of the scholarship on princely states exist as case studies. These studies caution against generalizing about their history, and yet all of them offer some generalizations. Let me start by pulling some of these general propositions together.

What Do We Know?

There were about 560 of these states. Probably the smallest state was Naigawan in the Gangetic plains. At seven square miles, it was little more than a village. In fact, well over half the states, almost all of them in the formerly Maratha-ruled western India, was not much more than a cluster of villages each. At the other end, there were the six larger states: Hyderabad, Mysore, Travancore-Cochin (two similar states joined together in 1949), Baroda, Indore, and Gwalior. At 83,000 square miles, Hyderabad was larger than most British Indian provinces. In north-western frontier regions and eastern and northern Burma, large territories were governed by tribal councils. These territories, though clubbed with the princely states, were not governed by hereditary rulers.[1]

These states were distinct from British India by being independent rules. But in the capacity to rule most of them were weaker than a British Indian district, even the larger of the landlord estates (Fig. 7.1). The so-called king of Darbhanga, for example, commanded a territory of 2500 square kilometres and revenue that far exceeded that of most of the states. But the king was not an independent prince, only a zamindar created by the Permanent Settlement.

In matters of administration, most states maintained their bond with tradition. They were ruled by a coterie of palace insiders, drew their main income from directly owned land or Khalsa land, and spent most of their money on maintaining the palace. The economy was agricultural in most and left on its own. Where feudal lords held land, a large part of the revenue and military force was beyond the control of the palace. So was the system of law and justice. But things were changing between 1860 and 1940, in at least three ways. In varying degrees, all states took part in these three processes.

First, there was increasing acceptance of the idea of bureaucratic rule. Formally the government remained a despotism. But in practice, several states left governance to bureaucrats headed by a chief minister and even

Fig. 7.1 'Native Durbar' (1855–1862). This photograph of a royal court or durbar in session somewhere in Western India reminds us that, except for about five or six, the 500-odd princely states in India were little more substantial than the estate of a village landlord (© DeGolyer Library, Southern Methodist University, William Johnson photographs of Western India)

experimented with representative government. Second, they tried to centralize their authority. Again their capacity to do so varied. In those states where feudal landlords retained their hereditary rights and power, the states could do little to increase their revenue. No state carried out thoroughgoing land reform. But they passed laws and experimented with alternative sources of revenue, and discussed a state-directed economic development of their domains more readily.

Third, while the states struggled to gain power, the globalization process reached their territories. Most states in the late nineteenth century understood by economic prosperity a concept very similar to how British

India saw economic development, the growth of commerce and cultivation. Railways and irrigation were the key instruments. Both challenges were more difficult to meet in the states, the majority of their land being hilly, dry, and without perennial rivers. When possible, they built railways and joined them with the network of lines that connected the port cities of British India. Neither industrialization nor investment in education or healthcare was a clear priority in the nineteenth century.

There were, however, a few exceptions to this pattern. In Travancore, state intervention focused on education. And Baroda, linked with Bombay and Ahmedabad by train, shared in the textile-based industrialization that was in full swing in these cities. Three states, Mysore, Baroda, and Travancore, where some of these strategies succeeded more than their neighbours, are often marked out from the rest and called the 'progressive' states.[2] I will suggest later that their progressive credential is overrated.

How well or badly did the states *on average* compared with British India? This is a tough question to answer because most states did not keep good records of economic activity, let alone publish these. Population and employment data, however, are of good quality, because these were collected by the Indian censuses. Let us start with that data.

British India and the Princely States Compared

John Hurd II processed census data to show that in the early twentieth century, the states lagged British India on three benchmarks, proportion of employment outside agriculture, the rate of migration, and urbanization. He attributed their poorer record on non-agricultural activity to the refusal of British India to guarantee princely state loans (which reduced capital expenditure) and the feudal structure of the states. Excessive influence of landlords reduced the freedom of the kings.[3]

Employment and urbanization are indirect and unreliable measures of economic change. We need more direct measures of comparison. In national income trends, the states did not show a distinct pattern of change from British India. I base this conclusion on the data for Figs. 1.1 and 1.2 (Chapter 1), which *include the princely states.* Going by this result, the states took part in business growth, mortality decline, and a stagnant rural sector. Income data for the states (Fig. 1.1), however, are of worse quality than population data (Fig. 1.2).

Another useful source allows us to compare the states and British India, only for one year (1908), but in much greater detail. The 25-volume Imperial Gazetteer of India collected a lot of information on regions. The Imperial Gazetteer did not set out to collect statistical information. But it used a uniform questionnaire in its descriptions of territorial units so that it is possible to pick from the descriptions, numbers relating to the area, population, revenue, rainfall, cultivated and irrigated areas, roads and railways, literacy, and the size of the largest town. From this dataset, partial or full details are available for 430 districts of British India and 130 princely states, covering 97% of the population and 93% of land area.[4]

The data reveals a few small differences in the conditions of the two types of territory. British India had a higher population density (rows 1–3 of Table 7.1) because it ruled over the coasts, the deltas, and the Indo-Gangetic Basin, the most fertile and populated regions of South Asia. The Company state in India began in the deltas and the coasts because it had been set up by the maritime merchants who had operated in the deltas and the coasts. These zones also had higher agricultural yield and richer states. On the other hand, a large part of the arid lands, deserts, forests, and dry uplands of the Deccan Plateau fell within the domain of the princely states (see rows 4 and 5 in Table 7.1).

This basic geographical difference led to a few other differences. One of these was the fiscal capacity of the states or districts (rows 6–8 of Table 7.1). Revenue in all cases came mainly (60–80%) from land, agriculture formed the principal livelihood. Given that the major part of the revenue came from land, an appropriate measure of the productive capacity of a region should be land revenue per cultivated area. The governments of the princely states were on average poorer if we measure revenue per acre. But given the higher population density in British India, revenue per head was smaller there. Also, princely states were relatively more dependent on non-land taxes (row 9 of Table 7.1), because they needed to compensate for their lower land tax.

Using this measure (tax-per-mile), we can test if British India and the princely states became more unequal over time or not because revenue-per-mile data are available also from an 1853 report.[5] A comparison of the two datasets suggests increasing regional inequality between 1853 and 1905. There was almost certainly a fall in inequality between 1905 and 1950, which we know because the statistical measure of regional inequality within the Indian Union reported immediately after

Table 7.1 British India and states, 1905

		British Indian districts (201)	*Princely states (198)*
1	Population, average per unit	968,764	318,865
2	Area, average per unit (square miles)	3891	3171
3	Population density	425	199
4	Cultivated area/total area (%)	52	20
5	Rainfall, annual (inches)	60	42
6	Total revenue per capita (Rs.)	2.05	4.34
7	Total revenue per square mile (Rs.)	425	386
8	Land revenue per square mile of cultivated area (Rs.)	1060	899
9	Proportion of non-agricultural to total revenue (%)	36	47
10	Roads (miles of paved road per 1000 square miles)	49.3	14.6
11	Railways (miles per 1000 square miles)	6.5	6.0
12	Size of the largest town as a ratio of population, per cent (size shown in bracket)	4 (38,634)	4 (13,334)
13	Literacy rate	4.3	3.5

Source India, *The Imperial Gazetteer of India*, vols. 1–31, Oxford, 1908. The figures are population-weighted or area-weighted averages as appropriate

independence in 1947 was significantly lower than what the 1908 gazetteer data would reveal to us. I will return to the rise and fall of regional inequality a little later.

The differences in geography and fiscal capacity translated into differences in infrastructure. There were few all-weather roads in the territory of the states (row 10, Table 7.1). In the heyday of railway expansion in India (1870–1920), the states built their own railways. Most served passenger traffic. In western India (such as Saurashtra in Gujarat), the states were so many and each so small that the state railways were built in small uncoordinated segments that did not feed effectively into the long-distance routes running through British India (row 11, Table 7.1, see also Fig. 7.2). Not surprisingly, the scale of urban settlements was smaller on average within the princely states (row 12, Table 7.1). Because

Fig. 7.2 The arrival of the first train in Alwar station, nineteenth-century. Princely states (like Alwar) emulated British India and built railways, hiring foreigners to run the system. With the small resources and territories that most of them had, the railways were usually short-haul narrow-gauge lines feeding into the main lines (© World History Archive/Alamy Stock Photo)

urbanization was limited, investment in schools was also limited, though, in respect of literacy (row 13, Table 7.1), princely states and British India were roughly similar.

The biggest cities in this time were the port cities. The four major ports, Bombay, Calcutta, Madras, and Karachi, were all located in British India. Among the larger princely states, only Travancore-Cochin had a long seafront. The economy of the two states was also more export-oriented, a fact helped by a rich maritime tradition. Of the other major states, Baroda was well-connected by rail with the Bombay port. But nearly all the others were land-locked and had no comparable history of long-distance commerce by sea.

Now consider some other differences between the two territories that Table 7.1 does not report on. Foreign investment inflow was significantly less in the states, with a few exceptions. The largest states (Mysore, Travancore, and Hyderabad) received more foreign investment in mining, railways, and trade. In Hyderabad, the railways and the colliery received foreign capital. In Mysore, the Kolar gold-fields, the single largest modern enterprise in the state, were foreign-owned. In Travancore-Cochin, plantations had a significant foreign presence.

But little foreign investment entered industrialization in the princely states, compared with British India. Industries were set up mainly by indigenous land-owning groups like, in Baroda the Kanbis, or the Syrian Christian community of Travancore-Cochin. In Indore and Gwalior, enterprise and capital in the textile industry mainly came from north Indian merchant communities like the Marwaris.

Next, consider government expenditure. Here there were two basic differences. In British India, the major expenditure was the maintenance of an army. In effect, the army guaranteed peace also in the princely states. By the terms of their agreement, British India would come in the aid of a princely state if one of them was attacked by another state. The princely states needed to keep small armies to maintain peace on their borders, an implicit subsidy delivered by British India. Usually, the biggest item of expenditure in the states was 'palace expenses,' that is, the upkeep and maintenance of the royal household.

A second difference in their fiscal systems was that few princely states borrowed from the market, whereas the Government of India did on a large scale to fund capital expenditure. The states were not encouraged to raise foreign sovereign debt, whereas British India could. British India feared that it might need to guarantee loans raised in London on behalf of states that did not have the capacity to take large foreign loans. Most states could not approach the London money market on their own anyway.

In running the financial system and the fiscal system, the British Indian government and the capitalists enjoyed greater access to the London money market than did their counterparts in the princely states. The Government of India security was a major financial instrument in London. Foreign capitalists in the late nineteenth century sold shares in London. Railway companies in the mid-nineteenth century raised capital in London. Balancing these inflows, there were also vast outflows of factor payments, debt service, and government remittances. This outflow the nationalists called drain, as we have seen. The princely states did not see such outflow. By its reluctance to sponsor the states' public debt, British India sheltered them from the so-called drain.

There was one similarity in the budgets of the two zones. Both zones understood well the dangers posed by over-reliance on the land tax, especially in times of famine when the land tax fell and the state needed money for famine relief. The dependence on land tax was reduced and that of commodity taxes and state royalties or excise increased. The chance to collect more money in this way was somewhat brighter in the South Indian states that had mines and plantations. In Mysore, the share of income from excise, forest royalties, state railways, and royalties from the Kolar gold mines increased substantially between 1880 and 1910. Forest income was also crucial in the numerous sub-Himalayan states.

Travancore scored a significant success in raising revenue in this way. To see this, compare Travancore's finances with those of its neighbouring Indian province, Madras, around 1901–1904 (I draw the data from V. Nagam Aiya's *Travancore State Manual*, p. 645 and *Statistical Abstracts for British India*, 1901–1904).

Revenue/head, Madras: Rs. 1.24
Revenue/head, Travancore: Rs. 2.71
Revenue/square mile, Madras: Rs. 340
Revenue/square mile, Travancore: Rs. 1516

Travancore had greater financial resources because it had a different economic structure from neighbouring Madras. In the former, the state earned an income from the assessment of plantation land, lands growing tree crops, from pepper monopoly, and was not too dependent on taxes that were taken from the peasants. In this respect, a more appropriate comparator for Travancore was not British India, but British Ceylon, both states had similar revenue earning profile. Interestingly, both states also had a better record than British India in welfare expenditure. They had more money to spare.

The increased earning was spent on infrastructure development. In the late nineteenth century, the main item of expenditure in both zones was the railways and irrigation. Reflecting geographical differences, British India could build more large-scale canal projects than could the princely states. But where possible, states took part in canal projects. The co-funded Sirhind canal on the Sutlej, for example, irrigated lands in Ferozepur and Ludhiana districts of British Punjab, and lands in the princely states of Jind, Patiala, and Nabha. Travancore did not need to spend money on canals. It was already a well-watered region and had a different crop regime from north India. It spent money on education instead. In the 1850s, when the education drive began, the state relied on the partnership of the Christian missions. Later it took on some of the financial burdens upon itself. In this way, a combination of Christianity and greater state capacity led to a literacy drive that made this region way more educated than the rest of India at the time of independence.[6]

Let me now return to the point about the rise in regional inequality in 1853–1905 and (possibly) a fall in 1905–1947. The explanation touches on the basic pattern of economic change in South Asia during these time-spans.

The Pattern of Economic Change

The nineteenth-century globalization, together with initial differences in geographical endowments, favoured British India more than the princely states. This globalization relied on the ports for export, the deltas and the Indo-Gangetic Basin for production of the commodities that went into trade, and foreign money raised by debt and investment to fund railways and irrigation. In all three respects, British India was better-endowed than were the states. These conditions, therefore, led to increasing inequality between British India and the princely states. Table 7.1 gives us a snapshot of how much the states fell behind. At the same time, most states emulated that model, with more limited resources, rather than pursuing a radically different pathway.

In the interwar period, two things reversed the relative position of the two zones. First, the British Indian pattern of growth came under stress in the 1930s. Cultivable land ran out, and agricultural commodities were not hot items in the world market. Industry and trade were both doing worse in the 1930s. Such adverse trends would affect British India more because it traded agricultural commodities more. The governments of both the states and British India tried to raise more money in the 1930s. In this effort, British India was more successful because it had bigger ports and could raise customs revenue. S. Sivasubramonian's national income calculations show that in 1921–1941, real income per person generated by the government more than doubled in British India, and nearly doubled in the states. But British India, with its military expenditure commitment, had a smaller capacity to spend on other heads.

Second, the concept of development changed. Nationalist criticism that the colonial state had neglected industrialization and welfare and the example of Soviet socialism made state leadership in industry and education more of a priority than it had been before. Both British India and the states tried to deliver more on these heads. The larger states could spend more.

In the interwar period, some of the larger states began to play a more active developmental role. In Mysore, there was much interest and commitment towards industrialization under the initiative of the state. In Mysore, Hyderabad, and Travancore, the government played or wanted to play, an active role in initiating industrialization. In Mysore, discussions about state aid to industry turned into a debate between two approaches, one focused on adapting traditional industry to modern markets and consumption patterns, and another on capital and intermediate goods under state sponsorship. The second approach identified with the Mysore Prime Minister (Diwan) M. Visveswaraiya won the debate. In the early twentieth century, a gold-field, cigarette factories, textile mills, and a steel factory were started in the public and the private sectors. Mysore's terrain and the many rivers had alerted the policy-makers to hydroelectric potentials. Bangalore was possibly the first major town to be illuminated by electricity. Hyderabad confined itself to industrial development under the leadership of the local landed and trading communities. But even here, the state gave direct and indirect encouragement to industrialization.

Some princely states compensated for the limitations of their financial system by sponsoring banks. The Bank of Baroda was started in 1908 by the Maharaja of Baroda, Sayajirao Gaekwad, in collaboration with the leading shroff houses of Baroda. Hyderabad pioneered the concept of state-backed investment banking, which was used by governments in post-independence India.

Although smaller than their counterparts in British India, the capitals of almost all princely states, small or large, saw new schools, colleges, in some cases, universities appear in the early twentieth century. There was a similar clustering of schools and hospitals in the British Indian district towns too, but the development in the states usually received personal attention by the ruling elites in contrast with the situation in British Indian districts.

The divergence was of a small order. The states did not as a whole experience a strikingly better economic path. That they did not is a puzzle. If colonialism was bad for economic development, surely independence would be good for development. Why, then, did the states fail to be significantly better than British India (compare revenue/head or revenue/sq mile in Table 7.1)?

Did Independence Matter?

The question can be answered in several ways. For example, independence might make the states *more willing* to play a developmental role.

A recent scholarship assumes that this must have been the case. Independence did make the states more development-minded, more inclined to spend on public goods, whereas the weight of colonialism made the British Indian provinces less willing or able to spend on infrastructure and welfare.[7] The argument is not persuasive. It overlooks state capacity. Their independence from British India notwithstanding, the princely states' capacity to design an autonomous development policy was constrained. There were three types of constraints.

One of these was colonial interference, such as the embargo imposed on raising loans in London. Individual projects designed in the states invited colonial interference, sometimes to the detriment of the project and the states concerned.[8] Such interferences did happen, though any claim that the states could do much better without British India poking its nose is far-fetched. Most states were simply not creditworthy. Further, colonial interference was not uniformly bad for them. The British Indian army subsidized the states' military expenditure. If British India interfered in the states' affairs, sometimes against their interest, there was also significant collaboration. The Sirhind canal in the north and the administration of Mysore are examples of such collaboration. So, colonialism was not necessarily a constraint on the capacity of the princely states.

The second type of constraint was internal. A feudalistic political structure, where much wealth and power rested with the landlords, made the kings weaker and left them less room to design and fund developmental projects.[9] Confirming this link in a different way, in Baroda, a deficiency of landlords made the court freer to act. Overall, the evidence to support or dispute this hypothesis is anecdotal.

My explanation combines geography and state capacity. The states were too resource-constrained to play the globalization game. The predominance of arid, upland, land-locked, and forest zones in their domain made them less able to promote trade by building railways and ports. They on average earned less money per square mile than British India. Even though they earned more money per head, most of the states were simply too small to make use of the economies of scale that large-scale projects would deliver. For example, the railways they built were too small and too few.

The exceptions to this rule were the so-called 'progressive' states—Mysore, Baroda, Travancore, and to a lesser extent, Hyderabad. These states thought about big projects, and about the state's role in shaping development. Baroda set up banks, Travancore invested in education, Hyderabad constructed railways, and Mysore went for industrialization and electricity. These states are called progressive to imply that they were more enlightened and more developmental, a propensity that must have come from their independence.

This is a wrong reading of the situation. Whether these states were more enlightened or not is irrelevant. They thought in developmental terms because they could. Princely states did not have to worry about funding an army, British India took care of that huge burden on their behalf. Compared with the other states, these four had the advantage of scale. They earned enough money and commanded big enough territories to undertake projects that involved economies of scale, like dams, railway, power stations, banks, and roads. It was their size that made them think differently. Economic structure mattered too. For example, the chance to collect more money in South India from mines and plantations was an advantage. These were cheaper taxes to collect than a tax on peasants. In 1905, the revenue per head of Mysore, Travancore, and Baroda was double that of British India, and the revenue per square mile was three times that of British India.

Conclusion

The message of this chapter is that the princely states were not strikingly different from British India in the nineteenth century. Both zones understood by economic progress the same thing—the growth of commerce aided by railways and canals. Princely states were constrained by geography, state capacity, lack of access to big capital markets, and small scale of units, to play that game as much as did British India. Whether they were independent or dependent had little relevance to how they defined progress or what they did to achieve progress.

The interwar years saw a convergence. In both zones, progress now meant state-aided industrialization and welfare. A few large states were more able to do this than was British India, where the globalization-led change was coming under stress and the still heavy burden of military expenditure left little money to spare.

Notes

1. For a descriptive history, see W. Lee-Warner, *The Native States of India*, London, 1910. See Barbara Ramusack, *The Indian Princes and Their States*, Cambridge: Cambridge University Press, 2008, for an analytical history.
2. See Ramusack, *The Indian Princes and Their States.*
3. John Hurd II, 'Some Economic Characteristics of the Princely States of India, 1901–1931,' PhD thesis of University of Pennsylvania, 1969. These hypotheses were re-examined by others with different data and results.
4. More on the data, Tirthankar Roy, 'Geography or Politics? Regional Inequality in Colonial India,' *European Review of Economic History*, 18(3), 2014, 306–323. The raw dataset is available on request from the author.
5. Anon, *The Native States of India* (Pamphlet), London, 1853.
6. Robin Jefferey, ed., *People, Princes and Parmount Power: Society and Politics in the Indian Princely States*, Delhi: Oxford University Press, 1978.
7. Lakshmi Iyer, 'Direct Versus Indirect Colonial Rule in India: Long-Term Consequences,' *Review of Economics and Statistics*, 92(4), 2010, 693–712.
8. See discussion in Ramusack, *The Indian Princes and Their States*, 186–204.
9. Hurd, 'Economic Characteristics.'

Further Reading

Barbara Ramusack, *The Indian Princes and Their States*, Cambridge: Cambridge University Press, 2008.

CHAPTER 8

Conclusion

Abstract History has a contemporary relevance for emerging economies. As in the past, in the present times too, globalization has unleashed extraordinary levels of capitalistic energy while leaving many livelihoods poor, stagnant, and discontented. This paradox of emergence connects two episodes of globalization in India a century apart.

Keywords Globalization · Economic inequality · Regional inequality · Democracy · Relevance of history

The book set out to write a report card on British India, reporting on its successes and failures as a state and as an economic system. It is time to announce the result. In one sentence, this is it: Colonialism and globalization helped businesses grow, reduced deaths, left the countryside poor, and by some benchmarks made the women worse off.

The achievements were enormous. Doing business was a struggle in nineteenth-century India. Interest rates were high, capital markets and capitalistic institutions were undeveloped, politics was often unfriendly. Why did capitalism work at all where capital was expensive, many skills were in short supply, and institutions were weak? At the end of the nineteenth century, India had one of the world's highest

© The Author(s) 2019

T. Roy, *How British Rule Changed India's Economy*,
Palgrave Studies in Economic History,
https://doi.org/10.1007/978-3-030-17708-9_8

infant mortality rates and lowest life expectancy at birth. Between 1900 and 1950, infant mortality halved, life expectancy doubled, and population growth rate increased from 0.1% per year in 1891–1901 to 1.2% in 1941–1951.

The colonial state did not set out to do any of this. It had no announced policy to develop India, nor did it command much money. It seemed to believe that allowing globalization and British science free play would solve India's problems. If the world economy was healthy, and Britain had a lead in science, the strategy might deliver results. It did deliver results. Businesses grew, and people lived longer. Indigenous entrepreneurship was already developed and partly global when colonial rule began. This indigenous resource met European science and enlightenment with a dramatic outcome.

And yet, globalization, capitalism, and science failed to offer solutions to India's agricultural problem, low and stagnant land yield. Markets and technologies did not make Indian society more equal either. The state had neither the means nor the stomach to do anything about social inequality. Between 1860 and 1940, most peasants were poor, many landlords were becoming poor, and forest-dependent people, pastoral people, and agricultural labourers lived as always in degrading poverty and owned neither land nor any other asset. Women were short-changed both in the work-place and at home. They had to manage larger families and retreated from paid work and industrial work in large numbers.

Such was history. Does history matter? Does the past explain the present? How different was India after independence (1947) from India in the colonial times? What was different? Were lessons learnt from the successes and failures of British rule in India?

In the field of economics, independent India took a step backward. Partly driven by xenophobia and partly by a fetish for socialist industrialization, India dismantled the open economic system that had emerged in the previous century. Commodity trade was banned, regulated, and nationalized. Private enterprise in finance was banned, regulated, and nationalized. Foreign trade and investment fell rapidly in importance. Global business firms, such as those in Calcutta, were allowed to be taken over and destroyed by opportunistic and incompetent Indian businesses. Transactions in science and technology were controlled by the government, which starved private enterprise of knowledge. Taxpayers' money was invested in manufacturing enterprises much of which proved unprofitable and pointless in the long run. The economy lost the capacity to pay for import by exporting, as a series of balance of payments crises showed.

If postcolonial India misread and ignored colonialism's successes, it learnt three useful lessons from its failures.

The first difference occurred in politics. The Indian Union after 1947 built a stable democratic system with universal franchise. In principle, only democratic states can have formal institutions through which the awareness of inequality and poverty can articulate and energize politics into acting. The British in India did not have these institutions and delayed their making. Second, social welfare received priority. Given the scale of inherited social inequality, the postcolonial successes in this field may seem too little. As writings by demographers and influential pieces written by Amartya Sen and his associates have shown, the conditions of women and girls did not improve as much as expected. But the record on welfare was still better than that of the colonial era. Third, the nation-state took bolder and more successful steps in improving agricultural technology, as the successive Green Revolutions showed. It used the taxpayers' money to do this, but that was a good use of the taxpayers' money in my view.

From the 1980s, India began to accept openness once more, allowing foreign trade and investment to play a larger role in the economy. By the 2000s, the economy had regained the capacity to pay for imports by exporting, which it had in the colonial times, though the basket of goods and services traded with the world was now vastly different from what it was in 1920.

The revival of capitalism and globalization revived a long-forgotten worry about inequality. These two forces can deliver great income-growth and yet leave these benefits concentrated in a small part of the economic system. Observe India today. What we should see are hubs of private enterprise that are wealthy, innovative, institutionally advanced, and rapidly improving in living conditions against the backdrop of a poor countryside that is changing slowly, even regressing by some benchmarks. The past looked exactly like this. Hubs of dynamic, wealthy, innovative capitalists did business in the backdrop of a poor countryside and a society that shut out some castes, some classes, and most women from the gains of trade.

By integrating India more closely with a Britain-centred world economy, colonial rule enabled a burst of enterprise. But such enterprise was largely an urban phenomenon. So is the present-day globalization process. It is emphatically a big-city phenomenon. There were remarkable parallels between the most dynamic business towns in the past and those in the present. Both tended to be cosmopolitan, outward-looking, globally connected places. Wealthier people and the middle class in both eras placed a lot of value on education and on technology. They traded with the world. Whether they exported textiles in 1750, wheat and cotton in 1850–1930, or software in 2010 is a point of detail.

India in the 1800s and India in the 2000s both had features of emerging economies—a poor country with a growing business sector. India's emergence in the former times was not an entirely happy story. Nor is emergence in the present times. Indeed, the ongoing emergence in India has sharply increased inequality between livelihoods, peoples, and regions. Women work more, and work further away from home, often taking enormous risk to their safety and well-being. Business growth in the colonial times similarly intensified inequality.

We should not overdo the equivalence between the two times. The difference between despotism and democracy is a fundamental one. Still, the fact remains that the Raj was good for business, and it was good for business for many of the same reasons that are working to further India's economic emergence now.

Index

A
Aden, 5, 6
Afghanistan, 30, 47
Africa, 5, 10, 16, 23, 47, 57, 104, 130
Agra, 30, 51
Ahmedabad, 51, 56, 58, 62, 69, 75, 139
Ambedkar, B.R., 18
America, 16, 20, 68, 82, 84, 113
American Civil War, 46, 82
Ananda Ranga Pillai, 48
Anstey, V., 18
Arabian Sea, 9, 31, 45, 47
army, 6, 9, 28, 34, 36, 38, 50, 59, 84, 101, 102, 104, 114, 115, 130, 135, 143, 147, 148
Assam, 63, 64, 124
Awadh, 28, 35, 50

B
balance of payments, 103, 153
bankers, 5, 9, 10, 28–30, 34, 36, 47, 50, 58, 59, 61, 69, 72
banks, 2, 16, 57, 59–61, 72, 81, 87, 100, 104, 109, 146, 148
Baroda, 51, 61, 137, 139, 142, 143, 146–148
Bay of Bengal, 47
Benares, 30, 41, 42
Bengal, 1–4, 9, 13, 22, 26, 28, 30, 31, 34, 37–39, 41, 47, 49, 60, 62, 63, 75, 83, 86, 87, 89, 95, 103, 117, 118, 123–125, 128–132
Berar, 87
Bhatias, 47, 69
Birla, 70, 72
Bombay, 9, 15, 19, 43–45, 47, 49–52, 56–58, 60–62, 65, 67, 70, 73–75, 82, 87, 115, 119–121, 132, 139, 142
British Empire, 5, 19, 21, 26, 33, 72, 109, 130
brokers, 36, 57, 63
Burma, 57, 70, 83, 122, 128, 137

© The Editor(s) (if applicable) and The Author(s), under exclusive licence to Springer Nature Switzerland AG 2019

T. Roy, *How British Rule Changed India's Economy*, Palgrave Studies in Economic History,
https://doi.org/10.1007/978-3-030-17708-9

C
Calcutta, 9, 15, 30, 34, 41–43, 48–51, 56–58, 60, 62, 63, 67, 69, 70, 73–75, 87, 101, 116, 142, 152
calico, 32
canals, 38, 83–86, 97, 120, 121, 144, 148
caste, 18, 47, 70, 72, 73, 87, 90, 91, 121
Central Asia, 5, 30, 47
Chettiars, 61, 70
Chettis, 47
China, 9, 15, 33, 42–44, 57, 62, 63, 68, 69, 83
China trade, 62, 63, 69
Cochin, 32, 43, 57, 137, 142, 143
Coimbatore, 62
colonialism, 20, 151
cotton, 45, 46, 57, 65, 69, 72, 76, 86
cotton textiles, 13, 31, 65, 66
currency, 6, 39, 60, 100, 101, 103, 107–109

D
Deccan Agricultural Relief Act, 93
Deccan Plateau, 2, 26, 27, 83, 86, 140
Delhi, 11, 21, 22, 30, 38, 51, 52, 79, 109, 110, 132, 149
diseases, 2–4, 16, 112–115, 118
Drain, 103
dubash, 47
Dutt, R.C., 2, 5, 17, 74, 120
Dwarakanath Tagore, 49

E
East India Company, 7, 9, 31, 33, 34, 48, 52, 103, 113
education, 15, 21, 40, 41, 47, 56, 67, 72–75, 79, 105, 112, 122, 124, 139, 144, 146, 148, 154
environment, 119
Europe, 7, 10, 14, 16, 20, 22, 31, 36, 45, 57, 68, 76, 84, 112, 113, 122, 130
European traders, 31, 32, 34, 48
exchange rate, 39, 107

F
famine, 2–5, 7, 8, 12, 16–19, 21, 26, 40, 75, 83, 86, 87, 92–94, 97, 106, 111–121, 125, 126, 128–132, 144
Foreign investment, 142
free trade, 107

G
Gandhi, M.K., 18
GDP, 52, 106
globalization, 5, 10, 16, 17, 19, 21, 78, 120, 138, 145, 147, 148, 151–154
Godavari, 26, 38, 85
Gold Exchange Standard, 108
Great Depression, 72, 82, 106
Gujarat, 26, 31, 47, 58, 87, 141
Gujarati, 33, 58, 61, 69, 93
Gwalior, 30, 137, 143

H
handicrafts, 5, 13, 14, 29, 30, 46, 72, 76, 90
handloom, 14, 62, 76, 118
Home Charges, 102, 107
Hong Kong, 5, 6, 43, 57
Hyderabad, 28, 34, 137, 142, 146, 148

I
income tax, 101, 102
Indian Ocean, 31, 34, 43

India Office, 6, 100, 101, 107, 108
indigo, 15, 29, 41, 48, 49, 56
Indo-Gangetic Basin, 5, 26, 28, 30, 41, 47, 83, 95, 119, 140, 145
Indore, 137, 143
industrialization, 7, 8, 11, 14, 15, 22, 62, 65, 70, 78, 122, 125, 139, 143, 145, 146, 148, 152
Industrial Revolution, 10, 13, 25, 82
inequality, 11, 17–20, 91, 94, 140, 145, 152–154
Infant mortality rates, 16
intellectuals, 5, 20, 40, 73, 74, 76, 115
Iran, 30
iron, and steel, 65

J
Jagat Seth, 47
Jamsetjee Jejeebhoy, 74
Japan, 57, 62, 66, 68, 83, 122, 128, 130
Jind, 144

K
Kanpur, 51, 56, 62
Karachi, 51, 56, 58, 86, 142
Kerala, 31, 32, 57, 90, 114
Khatris, 30, 47
Khojas, 47, 69
Komatis, 47
Konkan, 67
Krishna, 26, 38, 85

L
landless labourers, 91
landlords, 20, 28, 29, 38, 51, 58, 60, 74, 81, 87, 89, 95, 138, 139, 147, 152
Land revenue, 101
life expectancy, 3, 19, 131, 152
literacy, 15, 122, 124, 140, 142, 145
Lohanas, 47
London, 5, 6, 21, 22, 33, 36, 37, 44, 48, 63, 69, 98, 100, 101, 104, 106–110, 130–132, 143, 147, 149

M
Macaulay, T.B., 40, 41, 73
Madras, 9, 34, 38, 39, 44, 50, 51, 56–58, 60, 70, 87, 91, 97, 98, 119, 121, 142, 144
Madurai, 30, 62
Malabar, 19, 26, 31, 47, 57
managing agency, 71
Manchester, 7
Maratha, 34, 50, 87, 137
marriage, 18, 59, 70, 112, 122–125
Marwari, 30, 43, 47, 49, 61, 70, 93, 143
Marxism, 20, 90, 94
Masulipatnam, 32
Mayo, K., 18, 127
McAlpin, M., 3, 4, 120, 121
Merchants, 5–7, 9, 10, 15, 19, 21, 26, 28–31, 33, 34, 36, 40, 42–44, 46–51, 57–59, 61, 69, 72–75, 81, 94, 97, 102, 130, 140
middle-class, 14, 124
migration, 5, 10, 17, 34, 67, 92, 102, 118, 123, 139
missionaries, 44
moneylender, 2, 61, 92–94, 127
monsoon, 2, 17, 50, 59, 83, 87, 90, 117, 119
mortality, 3, 12, 13, 16, 105, 111–116, 121, 122, 125, 131, 139, 152
Moulmein, 43
Mughal Empire, 25–27, 30, 34, 36, 51, 52

Multan, 30
Mutiny, 5, 21, 50–52, 93, 101, 106
Mysore, 34, 115, 135, 137, 139, 142, 144, 146–148

N
Nabha, 144
Nagpur, 62
Naoroji, D., 5, 6, 17, 76, 103, 104, 110
Narmada Valley, 87
Natal, 5, 6
national income, 10, 12, 14, 22, 41, 59, 101, 103, 105, 106, 139, 145
nationalism, 17, 72
Northern Circars, 34

O
opium, 37, 41–45, 48, 56, 62, 69, 101, 102
Opium War, 43
Osaka, 57

P
Parliament, 36, 37, 93
Parsi, 43, 44, 48, 61, 69, 70, 74, 76
Patiala, 144
peasants, 10, 16, 17, 21, 28, 29, 37, 41, 58, 61, 67, 81, 82, 84, 87, 89, 90, 93–95, 97, 104, 109, 117, 118, 144, 148, 152
per capita income, 10–12, 28, 87, 105
Persian Gulf, 31, 47
Petit, 69, 74
Pondicherry, 34
population growth, 3, 12, 112, 113, 152
poverty, 2, 5, 16, 77, 81, 89, 92, 94, 95, 97, 102, 104, 124, 152, 153
princely states, 9, 15, 21, 35, 36, 102, 132, 135–148
Productivity, 13, 14, 22, 86
property right, 71, 95
protectionism, 41, 66
public debt, 6, 8, 104–106, 143
public health, 16, 19, 113–115
Punjab, 30, 34, 61, 84–87, 91, 93, 94, 97, 98, 144

R
Raichur Doab, 34
railways, 4, 6, 8, 13–15, 50, 55, 56, 58, 65, 69, 72, 78, 82, 85, 86, 92, 97, 102, 105, 112, 113, 120, 121, 139–142, 144, 145, 147, 148
Ralli, 57, 58
Red Sea, 31
religion, 18, 44, 47, 67, 69, 71, 123, 131, 143, 145
Royal Navy, 6, 33
Rustam Manock, 48, 52
ryotwari, 38, 87, 89

S
sardars, 67, 68
Sassoon, David, 57, 61
Sen, A.K., 129, 130, 132, 153
sex-ratio, 131
shipping, 30, 31, 33, 43, 47, 57, 72, 130
Sholapur, 62
Sind, 85, 117
Singapore, 57, 130
Spanish America, 33
spices, 30, 31, 57
Strachey, John, 2, 14, 17
Subarna Banik, 47, 49
successor states, 29, 30, 51

sugar, 29, 41, 48, 65, 66, 70, 85, 86, 131
Surat, 32, 33, 47, 48

T
Tagore, Rabindranath, 18, 123, 132
tariffs, 5, 62, 65, 66, 102, 107
Tata, 7, 57, 61, 65, 66, 69, 74
tea, 43, 49, 57, 63, 64, 69
technology, 4, 13–16, 19, 29, 33, 66, 72, 73, 79, 131, 152–154
telegraphs, 14, 105
transportation, 13, 26, 72, 78, 82, 83, 128
Travancore, 63, 137, 139, 142–144, 146, 148

U
United Provinces, 67, 97

V
Volkart, 57

W
wages, 13, 14, 17, 19, 67, 68, 77, 89, 91, 96, 103, 112, 122
wells, 83, 84, 97
West Asia, 31
women, 1, 11, 14, 18, 19, 40, 75, 77, 90, 112, 122, 124, 125, 131, 151, 153
World War I, 60, 63, 64, 72, 82, 101, 106, 107
World War II, 13, 66, 109, 117, 128
Wynaad, 63

Z
zamindars. *See* landlords